HEALING
is
God's Will
For You

By
Marge Pallett

Dedication

This book is dedicated first of all to Jesus Christ, my Savior, Lord and Healer. This book is also dedicated to all who need to know Jesus as their Healer or who need His healing touch. It is especially dedicated to all those who have been deceived by their enemy, Satan, into believing that God does not want them well body, soul and spirit, or that His healing promises are only for a chosen few.

Acknowledgements

I would like to express my deep appreciation to my dear friend, Ava Fisher, for her constant encouragement, faithful prayers, and help in editing and also, to my precious daughter, Margie Waldrop, without whose help in editing and in formatting, this book would never had made it to the publisher. Heartfelt gratitude to my friend, Sandy Redfearn, for her ministry to me which helped to bring this writing forth and for providing a peaceful, quiet place for me to write and pray uninterrupted. Last, but not least, many thanks to my husband, Richard, for his patience with me, his prayers, his belief in me and for sacrificing his time with me so I could fulfill what God wanted me to do.

Table of Contents

Introduction. xi

Part One—God's Will In Healing

Chapter One --------New Testament Evidence 21
Chapter Two --------Old Testament Evidence 32
Chapter Three ------Healing in the Atonement 44
Chapter Four--------The Promise of Long Life. 60
Chapter Five --------The Fading of the Healing
                          Ministry. 68

Part Two—Hindrances To Healing

Chapter Six ---------Paul's Thorn
                          (II Corinthians 12:1-10) 79
Chapter Seven ------Paul's Thorn
                          (Galatians 4:13-16). 91
Chapter Eight-------Paul's Thorn
                          (II Corinthians 10:10) 100

Chapter Nine -------Sin 108

Chapter Ten ---------Unbelief. 117

Chapter Eleven -----Ignorance of Spiritual Warfare 130

Chapter Twelve-----Unwillingness to Let Go 141

Chapter Thirteen ---Our Way or God's Way? 144

Chapter Fourteen---Inherited Sickness? 154

Chapter Fifteen -----Sickness For God's Glory? 158

Chapter Sixteen ----What About "Faith Healers?" 163

Chapter Seventeen -Ultimate" Healing 174

Chapter Eighteen---God's Sovereignty. 180

Conclusion 185

Appendix — Recommended Reading 193

Introduction

For several years now I have observed with increasing concern the tremendous amount of sickness that is present in the Body of Christ. I know of few Christians who do not take medicine on a regular basis or have on-going treatments for some abnormal physical condition or chronic disease. Recently, my concern has been heightened by epidemics caused by natural disasters, plagues, rising health costs, and the increasing use of dangerous drugs that can have devastating, even fatal, effects on the body.

The Bible clearly teaches that Jesus came to bring salvation *and* healing to all whom would believe and obey His word and that He intended those same people to be instruments of healing to others as well. And I wonder—why then, do we not witness more physical healings in and through the Church than we do?

As I have studied these past several years what the scriptures have to say on this subject, I have concluded that the main reason we do not see more of this manifestation of God's power is the lack of sound Biblical teaching on the subject of healing within the Church. I would challenge the reader to try to recall when he has last heard a sermon or in-depth teaching on the subject of healing as taught in the Bible.

There is such confusion, disagreement and ignorance among Christians on this one subject that the church, on the whole, is like "a trumpet giving forth an uncertain sound" (I Cor 14:8) so that Christians do not know how to battle the sickness within their midst.

The Church is greatly divided on the subject of healing — even Christians within the same local congregation. They just do not all *"speak the same language"* when it comes to physical healing as taught in the Bible.

Some of the varied beliefs that Christians voice about healing are:

"God wants to heal everyone."

"God still heals sometimes but because He is sovereign, He randomly chooses those he heals."

"Supernatural healings and other miracles ceased with the death of the Apostles."

"God doesn't heal directly anymore because we now have such advanced medical skill and knowledge, He expects us to get our healing that way."

"Sickness is a blessing."

"Sickness is a curse."

"You shouldn't pray for healing, only that God's will might be done because you might be praying against God's will."

"You should always pray for healing because the Bible says that you have not because you ask not."

"Sickness is of God."

"Sickness is of the devil."

"What good is healing? The purpose of the Church is to save souls."

"Salvation is more important than healing. Salvation is the 'real' miracle."

"God can use you as a witness in your sickness."

"God can use you in a greater way if you are well.

"There's so much we don't know about healing; we should just accept whatever God brings into our lives and not question Him."

"When the Bible talks about healing, it doesn't mean physical healing, it means spiritual healing."

"I know someone who was very sick and that person was anointed with oil and prayed over and he died. So I don't believe in that stuff anymore."

"I know a very holy person who has a successful ministry who has a chronic disease and has not been healed, so I know it can't be God's will to heal everyone."

"I get turned off when people start talking about healing because there are so many 'supposed' healers out there who are just faking it and taking advantage of people. So I don't want anything to do with healers or healing ministries."

Christians, with their conflicting beliefs and attitudes about healing, are somewhat like the people who tried to build the tower of Babel. Their common language enabled them to work together in unity toward accomplishing a common goal. They would have succeeded, too, if their goal had been a righteous one. But when God saw that their purpose was evil, He *"...confused their language..."* which brought an end to their unity and their ability to fulfill their purpose (Genesis 11:1-9).

Thus it has been with the Church in the matter of healing. Only at this time, it is not God who has confounded our language—it is the enemy of our souls, Satan. He knows the purpose and destiny of the Church is just and righteous—to glorify God in doing the works of Jesus—and he hopes that in bringing confusion and division, he can destroy the unity of the Church and defeat her purpose. Sad to say, he has had some success.

The Church has failed to believe, teach and practice what the Bible says about healing and that failure has resulted in confusion and unbelief to the point that many sick Christians have *"fallen through the cracks,"* so to speak. Many Christians not only are unable to receive the healing they need from God, but they cannot pray the prayer of faith for others because they either do not believe that God wants to heal the sick one or they do not know what to believe.

No doubt many individual's battle with disease has been lost because of the presence of unbelief in the sickroom. It is interesting that on at least one occasion Jesus felt it necessary to remove the doubters from the sickroom before the needed miracle took place (Matt. 5:35-40). Matt. 13: 58 says that the presence of unbelief prevented Jesus from performing mighty works—not that unbelief *ever* renders God powerless but it does often hinder an individual's, or group's, ability to receive what God has for him, or for them.

When Christians all begin to *"speak the same language"* concerning what the Bible teaches about healing, their corporate faith will enable them to see many more people healed, not just in their churches, but through their witness and ministry to the world.

Paul said, in I Corinthians 1:10:

> *"Now I plead with you, brethren, by the name of our Lord Jesus Christ, that **ye all speak the same thing,** and that there be no divisions among you, but that ye be perfectly joined together **in the same mind and in the same judgment."***

Often, Christians say, *"Well, there's a lot we don't know about healing."* It is said with an attitude of resignation, as if they do not have the means or the responsibility or even the desire to find out more about this aspect of the gospel.

Nevertheless, God never intended that one just experience salvation and go no further in his knowledge of God and of spiritual things. He expects Christians to learn and to mature in the things of God—to understand all that He has provided for and planned for them and to grow in their faith until they are able to receive all that He has for them. That is the *"working out"* of *"your own salvation"* that Paul speaks of in Phil. 2:12.

While physical healing is not as important as the salvation of the soul, it is nevertheless one of the great benefits of salvation and very much an essential part of the gospel. Consequently, Christians need to learn all they can about it.

The Bible has a great deal to say about healing. Much can be learned just from what Jesus had to say about the subject and observing how He ministered healing to different individuals. As Christians grow in their knowledge of what the Word actually teaches, they will grow in their ability to receive healing, to retain healing, and to minister healing to others.

In this book, I have presented my own insights into Biblical truths about healing and I have given the scriptural references where they can be found. I have also included a few insights of several well-known and respected servants of God whose writings on the subject of healing have been very helpful to me.

In spite of the care I have taken to validate my statements with corresponding scriptures, I realize that not everyone reading this book will see all that I do in the word of God. Nevertheless, my hope, my prayer and my aim is that many reading this book will find a key in something I have shared that will result in his own healing.

Without a doubt, God wants His people whole in body, soul and spirit (I Thess. 5:23; III John 2).

Part One

God's Will
in Healing

Chapter One

New Testament Evidence

Many Christians do not even dare to ask God for healing for fear they are asking for something that is not in accordance with God's will. As beloved children of a loving Heavenly Father one does not need to fear asking Him for anything. The scriptures says that Christians are to come boldly before the throne of God and ask for help in time of need (Hebrews 4:16). James says that *"…you have not because you ask not"* (James 4:2). If one keeps asking God for something that is not His will, He will eventually let him know in a loving way and will not scold him for asking (James 1: 5). If one does know God's will for whatever he is asking, then he has God's promise that He will grant it to him and that one should expect to receive it (I John 5:14-15, Matt. 7:7-8).

How does one know whether or not it is God's will to heal him? Because He has said so in His written will, the Bible. He made His will concerning healing clear in the Old Testament and confirmed it in the New Testament through Jesus' words and actions. The Bible says that Jesus is God's eternal Word that *"... became flesh and dwelt among us..."* (John 1: 14). Colossians 1:15 and Hebrews 1:3 both say that Jesus is the express image of the invisible God, His Father. Jesus' name "Emmanuel" means "God with us" (Matt. 1:23). John 1:1 tells us that *"*in the beginning was the Word, and the Word was with God and the Word *was* God." and John 1:14 says *"the Word* (Jesus) was made flesh and dwelt among us.* " II Cor.5:19, tells us that "... God was in Christ, reconciling the world to Himself ..."

Jesus came into the world, not only to reconcile His children to the Father by dying on the cross for their sins, but also to demonstrate the nature and will of God in ways that they could see and understand.

Jesus' life and ministry, as well as God's concern, His will and His purpose for mankind, are clearly revealed in the Bible. Jesus was totally submitted and committed to teaching and doing His Father's will. Listen to what Jesus himself had to say:

> *I can of My own self do nothing. As I hear,*
> *I judge; and My judgement is righteous,*
> *because **I do not seek My own will but the***

will of My Father who sent Me. (John 5:30)

*For I have come down from heaven, **not to do My own will, but the will of Him who sent Me.** (John 6:38).*

*I must work **the works of Him who sent Me** ... (John 9:4).*

***If you had known Me, you would have known the Father also;** and from now on you know Him and have seen Him" (John 14:7).*

Do you not believe that I am in the Father and the Father in Me? The words that I speak to you, I do not speak in my own authority: but the Father who dwells in Me does the works. (John 14:10).

Jesus made it very clear, in these and other scriptures, that the things that He said, did and taught were the words, the works and the will of His Father. Acts 10:38 says that Jesus *"went about doing good and healing all who were oppressed of the devil, because God was with Him"*.

Although Jesus performed a few other types of miracles besides healing and deliverance, most of His ministry consisted of teaching, healing sick bodies and minds and casting out demons that were causing sickness. A careful study of the accounts of Jesus' ministry, fails to reveal one incident where anyone came to Jesus seeking healing and did not receive it. If there were such an incident, one could conclude that it is not always God's will to heal, but such a thing never occurred.

Here are some of the accounts of the healings Jesus performed.

Matt. 4:23-24 reads:

> *And Jesus went about Galilee, teaching in their synagogues, preaching the gospel of the kingdom, and healing **all kinds of sickness and all kinds of disease** among the people. Then His fame went throughout all Syria; and they brought to Him **all** sick people who were afflicted with various diseases and torments, and those who were demon possessed, epileptics, paralytics; and He healed them.*

Matt. 8:16, Luke 4:40:

> *When evening had come, they brought to Him many who were demon possessed. And He cast out the spirits with a word. And healed **all who were sick.***

Matt. 9:35:

> *Then Jesus went about all the cities and villages, teaching in their synagogues, preaching the gospel of the kingdom, and **healing every sickness** and **every** disease among the people.*

Matt.14:35-36, Mark 6:56:

> *And when the men of that city recognized Him, they ... brought to Him all who were sick and begged Him that they might only touch the hem of His garment. And **as many as touched it were made perfectly well.***

Matt. 15:30:

> *Then great multitudes came to Him, having with them the lame, blind, mute, maimed, and many others: and they laid them down at Jesus' feet, and **He healed them**.*

Mark 1:32-34:

> *At evening, when the sun had set, they brought to Him all who were sick and those who were demon possessed. And the whole city was gathered together at the door. Then He healed* **"many who were sick with various diseases, and cast out many demons ..."**

(The word *"many"* here does not imply that Jesus only healed *some* of the sick, only that many of the city's residents who were gathered around Jesus that evening were sick, so Jesus healed the many that were.)

Luke 6:17-18:

> *And He came down ... and a great multitude*

*of people ... came to hear Him and be healed
of their diseases, as well as those who were
tormented with unclean spirits and they were
healed. And the whole multitude sought to
touch Him, for power went out from Him and
He healed them **all.***

Luke 9:11:

But when the multitudes knew it, they fol-
lowed him; and He received them and spoke
to them about the kingdom of God, and
healed *those who had need of healing.*

Jesus also gave His twelve disciples (Matt. 10:1-8) and
the seventy (Luke 10:1, 8-9, 17) that same *"...power over
unclean spirits, to cast them out and to heal **all kinds** of
sickness and **all kinds** of diseases"* (Matt.10:1). He put no
restrictions on that power. It was to benefit all who would
receive the gospel (Luke 10:8-14). According to James 5:14-
15, the power to heal was also given to those elders in the
Church so they could pray the prayer of faith over those who
were sick.

(There was even one unnamed person who, the disciples

complained to Jesus, was casting out demons in Jesus' name and they wanted Jesus to stop the man from doing that because, as they said, he was not one of their group. Interestingly, Jesus refused to forbid the man to do what he was doing, saying that the man was *"on our side"* (Mark 9:38-40).

In Mark 16:15-18, the Bible says that Jesus gave the power to heal and cast out devils to *"he who believes"* among *"**every** creature"* to whom the gospel is preached. F.F. Bosworth, the well-known Canadian healing-evangelist of the late eighteenth and early nineteenth centuries, points out that every time Jesus commissioned someone to preach the gospel, He also gave them the power to heal. (p. 211)

Had Jesus been healing the sick and doing other miracles solely to prove that He was the Messiah (as some state), surely He would not have given this power to so many others, lest someone mistake the one He commissioned to be the true Messiah.

If God did not will for everyone to be healed, Jesus would have been acting contrary to His Father's will by healing them all and giving His disciples, the seventy (Luke 10:1), and all believers (Mark 16:17), the power to do the same, without any restrictions.

However, Jesus let it be known that some would not

believe the gospel and so would not receive its benefits (Matt.10:14, Luke 10:10). God cannot give to man that which man is unwilling to receive. Many times, it is *man's* own will that hinders him from receiving the blessings that God has promised. Jesus was revealing His will concerning healing to all men everywhere, for all time when He said to the leper who questioned Jesus' willingness to heal, *"I am willing!"* (Mark 1: 40-42).

James, the leader of the New Testament Church, whose wisdom was sought and readily received by the apostles and elders at the counsel in Jerusalem, gave these instructions to the growing Church:

> *Is **anyone** among you sick? Let him call for the elders of the church, and let them pray over him, anointing him with oil in the name of the Lord and **the prayer of faith will save the sick, and the Lord will raise him up.** And if he has committed sins, he will be forgiven (James 5: 14-15).*

One ought to give the same meaning to the word "anyone" here that is given to the word "whosoever" in John 3:16 and have the same expectancy of God fulfilling His Word! In fact, if one cannot believe that the *"anyone"* in James 5:14 means *all* who are sick, then one cannot believe that the *"whoso-ever"* in John 3:16 means anyone and everyone either.

If it were not God's will to heal all of His children, James 5:15 would have to read,

> *And the prayer of faith **might** save the sick, and the Lord might raise him up, and if he has committed sins, he **might** be forgiven.*

Who could pray the prayer of faith under those condi-tions? It would serve no purpose to anoint with oil if there were not some results to expect from doing so. God takes no pleasure in meaningless ritual. God's promises are never -*"maybe"* but *"yes"* and *"amen"* (II Cor.1:20).

What is the "prayer of faith?" Is James talking about a general faith—one that simply acknowledges the existence and sovereignty of God? No, because James is also the one who declares that even the demons have that much faith, yet one knows that it does not benefit them (James 2:19). The kind of faith that James is talking about is the kind of faith that believes that God will do all that He has said He will do *in any specific situation.* If one has that kind of faith, he will demonstrate it by meeting God's condition and expecting to receive what God has promised. When one does his part in obeying God's command, God always does His part in response to that obedience.

One method by which one can expect to receive healing is found in James 5:16 which says *"Confess your trespasses to one another, and pray for one another, that you might be healed."* This instruction, too, is for the Church and surely, James would not have given it to the Church if he did not believe that it was God's will for everyone to be healed.

Another important piece of evidence that God wants to heal His children is found in Matt. 15:22-28. Here Jesus called healing and deliverance the *"children's bread,"* (meaning a daily necessity). Further New Testament evidence will be presented in chapter three entitled *"Healing in the Atonement"*.

Chapter Two

Old Testament Evidence

In the book of Exodus, chapter 15, verses 22-26, God had brought the children of Israel out of the land of Egypt where they had been in bondage for over four hundred years. God had incredible plans for Israel. He intended to make them a channel through which He could demonstrate His sovereignty, His power, His will and His faithfulness to the rest of the world. However, He first must demonstrate to them what He purposed to do through them.

God showed His sovereignty, power and faithfulness through the plagues that came on Egypt and the bringing out of His people from that land. He further demonstrated these attributes in parting the Red Sea for them and destroying Pharaoh and his army.

Then He revealed His will concerning healing to His people at the waters of Marah. When the people found they could not drink the waters because the waters were bitter, they cried out to Moses who then cried out to God. God showed Moses a tree and commanded Moses to throw it into the water. When Moses obeyed Him, the waters *"became sweet"* (were healed).

As God healed the waters, He gave the Israelites their very first conditional promise:

> *... If you diligently heed the voice of the Lord, your God, and do what is right in His sight, give ear to His commandments and keep all His statutes,* ***I will put none of these diseases on you*** *which I have brought upon the Egyptians. for* ***I am the Lord who heals you*** *(Exodus 15: 26).*

In Exodus 23:25-26, He further says:

> *So you shall serve the Lord your God, and He will bless your bread and your water.* ***And I will take away sickness from the midst of you. No one shall suffer miscarriage or be barren in all your land; I will fulfill the number of your days.***

In Deut. 7:11-15, Moses reminds the Israelites of God's promise:

> *Therefore you shall keep the command-ments, the statutes, and the judgments which I command you today, to observe them. Then it shall come to pass, because you listen to these judgments and keep and do them, that the Lord your God will keep with you the cov-enant and the mercy which He swore to your fathers. And He will love you and bless you and multiply you: He will also bless the fruit of your womb and the fruit of your land, your grain and your new wine and your oil, the increase of your cattle and the offspring of your flock: in the land of which He swore to your fathers to give you. You shall be blessed above all peoples:* **there shall not be a male or female barren among you or among your livestock. And the Lord will take away from you all sickness, and will afflict you with none of the terrible diseases of Egypt which you have known, but will lay them on all those who hate you.**

In Deut. 11: 26, Moses again speaks for God when he says,

> *Behold, I have set before you today* **a blessing**
> **and a curse,** *the* **blessing, if you obey the**
> **commandments of the Lord your God** *which*
> *I command you today:* **and the curse, if you**
> **do not obey** *the commandments of the Lord*
> *your God, but turn aside from the way which*
> *I command you today: to go after other gods*
> *which you have not known.*

Then, in Deut. 28, verses 1-14, Moses lists many of the blessings that will come to those who are careful to obey the voice of the Lord. He gives an even longer list of curses that will come on the disobedient, among which are *various kinds of diseases* (verses 20-22, 27-28). The diseases named in verse 22 were probably those that were most common in that day. However, verse 61 tells us that the curse of sickness includes every sickness and every plague which is *"not written in the book of the Law."* This would include our modern day illnesses.

However, some Christians might say, *"This was the Old Testament and these were the Jews. What does that have to do Gentile Christians living today? What does that have to do with me?"*

Well, Timothy says, *"**all** scripture is given by inspiration of God, and is profitable for doctrine, for reproof, for correction, for instruction of righteousness..."* (II Tim. 3:16). In I Corinthians 10:1-11, Paul is talking to Gentile Christians about the Israelite's journey through the wilderness on their way to the promised land. He names some specific sins that the Israelites had committed and the destruction that came on them because of their sin. Those sins mentioned were idolatry (verse 7), sexual immorality (verse 8) and complaining (verse 10). Paul says in Verse 6:

> *Now these things **became our examples** to the intent that we should not lust after evil things as they also lusted.*

Verse 11 says,

> *Now all these things happened to them as examples, and they were written for **our admonition, upon whom the ends of the ages have come.***

Paul's admonition included everyone who would be living in the last days. He let the Gentiles know (in Gal. 3:7;

3:9; 3:14; Romans 11:7-24 and Eph. 2:11-20) that those who trust in Christ are also children of Abraham and as such are entitled to the spiritual blessings promised to Abraham's seed. As Israelites (in a spiritual sense), they are also subject to the same consequences (curses) of disobedience.

While the people of the Old Testament are real people and the events concerning them are actual historical events, the nation of Israel is also a type and shadow (or word picture) of the Church of Jesus Christ. The Israelites' deliverance from Egypt, journey to, and conquest of, the Promised Land (Canaan) is a type of the Church's deliverance from sin and their spiritual journey to entering into the promises of God through Christ. Egypt represents the bondage of sin in which all unbelievers are before they come to Christ.

The Promised Land for the Christian is not heaven per se, as many suppose, although it does include heaven. The *Promised* Land for the Christian is the *Promise* Land. It is the Land of the Fulfillment and Enjoyment of God's Promises, such as peace, joy, provision, safety, wisdom, etc., as well as physical healing for one's body.

The trials that Israel went through, and the enemies they met and fought along their physical journey, are a type of the spiritual forces of darkness that the Christian, too, can expect to confront on his *spiritual* journey. These enemies of righteousness—doubt, fear, murmuring, complaining, idolatry, ungratefulness, bad habits, bad attitudes, etc.—must be overcome if the Christian is to receive all that God has for him.

In Proverbs 3:7-8 and 4:20-22, God's promise is that those who heed (obey) the word of God shall find *"life"*, *"health for their flesh"* (bodies), and *"strength for their bones."*

In Isaiah, chapter 58, God tells His people that if they will fulfill His purpose for their lives, and cease doing those things that displease Him, their *health* will *"spring forth speedily"* (verse 8) and God will *"strengthen their bones"* (verse 11).

Psalms 34:19 declares:

> *Many are the afflictions of the righteous but the Lord delivers him out of them all.* According to the New Strong's Exhaustive Concordance of the Bible, the word *"afflictions"* here does not literally mean *"sickness"* but rather adversity, calamity, distress, sorrow, trouble, which of course could *include* sickness. (p. 21) The promise of deliverance is simply

to the *"righteous"*—those in right standing with God.

Of course, if the above scriptures have no significance for the Church, then Christians have no right to claim them or take comfort in them.

The same can be said for Ps. 103:1-5.

> *Bless the Lord, O my soul, and all that is within me bless His holy name. Bless the Lord, O my soul, and forget not all His benefits: Who forgives all your sins, who heals all your diseases, Who redeems your life from destruction, Who crowns you with loving kindness and tender mercies, Who fills your mouth with good things so that your youth is renewed like the eagles.*

David understood that God's covenant with Israel was an *assurance* policy that included many wonderful benefits—the forgiveness of *all* sins, the healing of *all* diseases, deliverance from evil, divine favor and renewed youth (vigor and vitality). Did this portion of scripture apply only to the Jews under the Old Covenant? If so, then present day Christians must cease to draw comfort and encouragement from it.

Some Christians would have one believe that all of this scripture (Psalm 103:1-5), applies to today's Christians except for the part about the healing of *all* our diseases, because they say that God grants healing to some people but not to others. If that is true, how can one believe that God forgives *all* of his sin?

Consider Psalm 91, another favorite Psalm of many Christians. This Psalm declares that the one who dwells close to God, under His wings (verse four), God will *surely* (without a doubt) *"deliver from the snare of the fowler and from the perilous pestilence"* (verses 1-3). (The word *"pestilence"* means a *"disease of epidemic proportions,"* according to the Random House Dictionary) Cancer, AIDS, heart trouble, diabetes, cancer, congestive heart failure, etc., are all diseases that have reached epidemic proportions in our society today).

Psalm 91 also declares that the one who takes refuge under God's wings shall be protected, *by God's word*, from even the *fear* of terror and disease, and other destructive things (verses 4-6). Verses nine and ten declare that those who make the Lord their dwelling place shall be protected from evil and from *any* plague coming near their dwelling.

Again, if the promises in this Psalm are not applicable to all in the body of Christ but only to *some* that God chooses to protect from plague and pestilence, how can it offer any solace or strength to anyone unless they know that they are a part of the *"some"*? If it *is* for everyone that makes up the Church today, why do some Christians not see its truths manifested in their lives? Do they not believe God's promises or are they failing to meet His conditions?

Malachi prophesied this about Jesus, *"Unto **you that fear My name** shall the sun of righteousness arise with healing in His wings..."* (Malachi 4:2). The healing virtue in Jesus' wings is not just something that He brings to believers. No, that healing is *resident* in Jesus because He *is* the Healer. Those healing wings are a covering for all those who fear His name enough to dwell (live consistently) in that place of close, unbroken fellowship. It obviously is impossible that healing and sickness could dwell together in the wings of Jesus.

God's purpose for the nation of Israel and His purpose for the Church is the same—to walk in close fellowship with God, to enjoy His many blessings, and to be a witness to the world of God's sovereignty, holiness, power and goodness. His methods in bringing this to pass may vary but His purpose has never changed...His nature has not changed either. In the Old Testament, God declared to Moses that He is the

41

I AM—not the I WAS or I WILL BE. God is God of the present and always will be. Jesus, being God in the flesh who dwelt among us, is also the great I Am. He is NOW whatever He was in the beginning and will be in the future. He has not changed. He will not change. He cannot change. If He did, he would be a liar and an imposter. In Malachi 3:6, God says:

"I am the Lord, I change not".

God's name(s) reveal His very nature. In the Old Testament, God revealed Himself to His people by several names, one of which was Jehovah-Rapha— *"I Am the Lord Who Heals You."* (Exodus 15:26). That means He is, was, and always will be the Lord who heals His people.

The apostle James says that there is *"no variation or shadow of turning"* with our heavenly Father (James 1:17). The writer of Hebrews declares that Jesus, who is the express image of the Father (Hebrews 1:3), is *"the same, yesterday, today and forever"* (Hebrews 13:8).

In the book of Acts, chapter 4, after Peter and John had healed the lame man at the gate of the temple and a crowd had gathered, Peter declared to them that it was by the *"name of Jesus"* that the man had been healed (verse 10). Then in verse 12, He lets them know that there is also salvation in the *"name of Jesus."*

Therefore, just as the Shulamite woman (a type of the Bride of Christ) in the book of The Song of Solomon (S. of S. 1:3) could declare that her lover's name was as *"ointment poured forth,"* those who know Christ (who is the lover of their souls) can declare that His name is "*as ointment poured forth*" because of the healing virtue that is in His name.

The Bible says in Acts 4:10, "*[L]et it be known to you all...that by the **name** of Jesus Christ...by Him this man stands before you whole.*" Jesus saves and heals because that is His nature—His identity. He is Savior and Healer and Deliverer. He has not stopped being who He was and is. The same power, compassion and provision for the physical needs of God's children are still resident in Jesus, who is alive, and they are available to all today who will believe Him for them.

Chapter Three

Healing in the Atonement

T he Bible clearly teaches that the atonement of Christ paid for the Christian's healing as Isaiah tells us, in chapter 53, verse 5, that Christ *"was wounded for our transgressions and by His stripes we are healed,"* attributing both our salvation and physical healing to Jesus' suffering and death. (The Hebrew word for "healed" used here is *"rapha"* which means to mend, repair, cure, cause to heal, physician, to make whole.) Isaiah also said, in verse four, "surely He has borne our *griefs* and carried our sorrows." Although the Hebrew word used here—*kholee*—has several meanings, most Bible scholars agree that the word, as used in this passage and others, is most accurately translated *"sicknesses."*

In Matthew 8:17, when Matthew talks about Jesus' healing of the sick being the fulfillment of Isaiah's prophecy, the Greek word *"nosos"* is used, which translates disease, infirmity, sickness:

*"When evening had come, they brought to Him many who were demon-possessed. And He cast out the spirits with a word and healed all that were sick, that it might be fulfilled which was spoken by Isaiah, the prophet, saying, 'He Himself took our infirmities and **bore our sicknesses.**"*

The last part of I Peter 2:24 reads: *"...by whose stripes you were healed."* Peter uses the Greek word *"iaomai"* for the word *"healed"* which means to cure, to heal, to make whole.

F.F. Bosworth, in his book, *"Christ the Healer"* has this to say:

"His [Christ's] present attitude is revealed in the very meaning of the word 'salvation.' The word, *soteria,* which is the Greek word for salvation, implies deliverance, preservation, healing, health, soundness, and, in the New Testament is applied sometimes to the soul and at other times to the body only. The Greek word, *"sozo"* translated "saved" also means "healed," "made sound," "made whole." In Romans 10:9, it is translated "saved," and in

Acts 14:9, the same word is translated "healed" in referring to the healing of the man lame from birth. Both Greek words for "salvation" and "saved" mean both physical and spiritual salvation; or, in other words, spiritual and physical healing. Paul, in Eph. 5:23 states, "He is the Savior of the body." (p. 70,71)

In Exodus, chapter twelve, when the Lord gave instructions to the children of Israel on observing this first Passover, He told them to kill a lamb (one without blemish) and put its blood on the doorposts and lintel of their homes. When the Lord came to bring judgment on Egypt, which was that the firstborn of every household would die, the blood on the Israelites' doorposts would signify that the occupants were God's people and they would be spared that judgment.

Why did the Lord do this? Did He not know who was His own and where they lived? Of course He did, but here He was giving His people a picture of the atonement of Christ and all that it would accomplish for mankind. The applying of the blood on the doorposts was not all that the Israelites were to do. They were also instructed to roast the lamb in the fire and eat every bit of it. The Bible does not say what purpose this served, but it was probably to ensure the strengthening of their bodies in preparation for the long, hard journey ahead. The body of the lamb evidently did bring that help and strength to them, as Psalm 105:37 does say, "*...there was not one feeble one among them*" when the Lord brought them out.

Some Christians believe that the roasted lamb, as well as the unleavened bread that they were told to take with them, was a type of the body of Christ that was broken (torn open, mutilated, *"roasted in the fire"*) for the healing and the strengthening of their bodies. Perhaps that is why Christ instructed His followers to take both the bread and wine in Communion—one element representing His blood shed for their sins, and the other (the bread) representing His broken (mutilated) body and the stripes by which they are healed.

Although Christ, or Jesus, is not mentioned by those names in the Old Testament, there are many shadows and types (symbols) of Christ given there. Jesus said, in Luke 24:44, that the books of Moses, the prophetic books and the Psalms all speak of Him.

The tree that was thrown into the bitter waters of Marah was also a type of Christ and His atoning work on the cross. This signifies that when Christ comes into an individual's life at salvation, His presence in that life is meant to bring healing to him.

It helps to understand that healing is provided for the

Christian in the atonement when one observes from the Bible the connection between sin and sickness and also the connection between repentance (turning from sin) and physical healing.

In the Old Testament, when God's people sinned against Him, He sent plagues to the people. However, when they repented of their sin, God stopped the plague. (Unlike the plagues of Egypt in the time of Pharoah which took various forms, those sent to the Israelites in the wilderness were usually those of sickness—Exodus 32:35; Numbers 11:33; Numbers 14:37; I Chron. 21:11-12, 14; Micah 6:13).

In Numbers 8:19, God said, *"And I have given the Levites as a gift to Aaron and his sons. . . to make **atonement** for the children of Israel, that there **be no plague** among the children of Israel... "*

Numbers 16:46-50 tells us that when the children of Israel rebelled against Moses and Aaron's leadership, God sent an earthquake *and* a plague to the people. When Moses and Aaron made atonement for the people, the *plague* stopped.

There is an account in Numbers 21:4-9 of an occasion where the children of Israel had been murmuring and complaining against both God and Moses. God became angry with the people because of their false accusations and ingratitude. Therefore, He sent fiery serpents among the people

48

that bit them so that many of them died of the snakes' bites. When those who were still alive confessed that they had sinned and asked for mercy, God gave Moses instructions to make a fiery serpent out of brass and put it on a pole. He said that everyone who looked at the pole would be healed of their snakebites and would live.

The pole was a type of the cross and the serpent on the pole was both a type of sin and also of Christ and His atoning work on the cross. Jesus Himself identified that fiery serpent as a type of Himself when He said, in John 3:14,

> *"As Moses lifted up the serpent in the wilderness, even so must the Son of Man be lifted up."*

II Corinthians 5:21 tells us that "He *made Him who knew no sin to be sin for us, that we might be the righteousness of God in Him."* Gal 3:13 reads:

> *"Christ has redeemed us from the curse of the law, having become a curse for us, for it is written 'cursed is everyone who hangs on a tree.'"* (in reference to Duet. 21:23).

In that day, the people of God looked to the serpent on the pole and were healed and/or delivered based on what Christ would one day accomplish on the cross. All who now *"look to Christ"* (Hebrews 12:2), who *"lift Him up"* by proclaiming Him as their Lord and Savior, receive salvation, healing and deliverance by His finished work on the cross.

David linked forgiveness of sin and healing of the body when he stated that both were benefits of salvation (Ps. 103: 1-3). The writer of Psalm 91 tells us that the one who lives close to God (free of sin) can expect immunity from plagues and pestilence.

The book of Proverbs states that forsaking of sin (repentance) and obedience to God's word will bring health to our bodies (Pro. 3:7-8, 4:20-22).

Isaiah 33:24 says:

"And the inhabitant shall not say *I am sick;* the people that dwell therein *will be forgiven their iniquity."*

The Lord prophecies through Micah 6:13, against the rebellious house of Israel,

> *"Therefore I will also make you **sick** by striking you, by making you desolate because of your **sins**."* (Micah 6:13).

Malachi prophesied that the One who came to bring salvation to mankind would also provide healing for those who feared Him enough to obey Him (Malachi 4:2).

In the account of Jesus' healing of the paralytic man in Mark 2: 1-11, the man had been brought by friends to Jesus in the hope that Jesus would heal him. Before Jesus healed him, He said to the man, *"Son, thy sins be forgiven thee."* Evidently the man's greatest need was for salvation and his sins needed to be forgiven before he could receive His healing.

After Jesus healed the man at the pool of Bethesda (John 5:14), Jesus said to him, *"Go and sin nor more lest a worse thing come upon you."* Whether the man's sickness was the direct result of a certain sin in his life or whether his sinful condition just made him vulnerable to whatever misery life (or Satan) handed him, is not clear. However, Jesus let him know that if he continued to indulge in sin, he would not only lose his healing but would be in worse shape physically than he was before the healing. In both of the above situations, Jesus makes a very clear connection between sin and sickness and forgiveness of sin and healing.

Then, of course, James makes the connection of sin to sickness and repentance to healing when he says:

> *"Is anyone among you sick? Let him call for the elders of the church, and let them pray over him, anointing him with oil in the name of the Lord. And the prayer of faith will save the sick, and the Lord will raise him up. **And if he has committed any sins, he will be forgiven. Confess your trespasses to one another, and pray for one another, that you may be healed"***
> (James 5:14-16).

The apostle Peter, in I Peter 2:24, makes reference to Isaiah's prophecy of Jesus, *"by whose stripes you were healed"* and ties that in with Jesus' dying for our sins:

> ***"Who Himself bore our sins in His own body on the tree, that we, having died to sins,*** *might live for righteousness ... by **whose stripes you were healed."***

Did the apostle Paul give any indication that healing was

provided for believers in the atonement? Well, Paul certainly did show the close connection between sin and sickness, and repentance and healing. Most Christians are familiar with the first few lines of Paul's instructions on how to participate in the Sacrament of Holy Communion in I Cor. 11:23-26:

"For I received from the Lord that which I also delivered to you: that the Lord Jesus on the same night in which He was betrayed took bread; and when He had given thanks, He broke it and said, 'take, eat; this is My body which was broken for you; do this in remembrance of Me.' In the same manner, He also took the cup, after supper, saying, 'This cup is the new covenant in my blood. This do, as often as you drink it, in remembrance of Me.' For as often as you eat this bread and drink this cup, you proclaim the Lord's death until He comes."

But Paul's instructions did not stop there, although one seldom hears them given in a church service on Communion Sunday. (And that is a shame, because some pastors will have to give account someday for withholding truth from their flock that could set them free.)

53

Paul goes on to say, in verses 27-32:

> *"Therefore whoever eats this bread and drinks this cup of the Lord in an unworthy manner will be guilty of the body and blood of the Lord. But let a man examine himself and so let him eat of the bread and drink of the cup. For he who eats and drinks in an unworthy manner eats and drinks judgment to himself, not discerning the Lord's body.* **For this reason many are sick and weakly among you and many sleep. For if we judge ourselves we would not be judged. But when we are judged we are chastened by the Lord, that we may not be condemned with the world."**

Paul was addressing a situation here where people had been celebrating the Lord's supper in a rude, disrespectful and selfish manner. Some were feasting while others were allowed to go hungry. They were failing to show love and consideration for their brothers and sisters in Christ. Some were actually using the occasion to get drunk.

What is worse, they were coming to the communion table

with a hypocritical attitude, as though there was nothing wrong with their behavior. They were making a mockery of everything the Lord's supper was meant to represent. They were not *"judging themselves"* by acknowledging their sinful attitudes and behavior and their need to be cleansed and changed.

Paul said that is the reason some of the people were weakly and sick and some "were asleep" (which means they had died). Paul said that when they ate and drank the communion elements in this sinful state, they damned themselves and came under God's judgment which was sickness or death.

That is why Paul admonishes all Christians to examine themselves before coming to the Lord's table, to see if there is any sin in their lives of which they need to repent. *Then,* when that is taken care of, *". . . let him eat of that bread and drink of the cup"* (verse 28).

In light of what Paul says, any Christian who has been suffering sickness as a chastisement for unconfessed sin in their life should expect that chastisement to be lifted as they take communion in humility and repentance—especially as they reflect on *all* that Christ's death has accomplished for them.

Many people have testified that they have experienced a physical healing, as well as a renewed sense of sins forgiven, as they have partaken of Holy Communion with a right attitude. That sacrament also, like the anointing of the sick with oil, was never meant to be an empty ritual, but a means of impartation of grace to those who have prepared their hearts to receive it.

Considering the context of the entire eleventh chapter, Paul's words, in verse 29, *"...not discerning the Lord's body."* most likely refer to the failure of some of these Corinthian believers to recognize and treat their fellow believers as also being members of Christ's body and worthy of honor and respect.

But, in light of other scriptures, it seems there is more than one way in which one can fail to *"discern the Lord's body."* If one does not understand or believe that Christ bore mankind's sicknesses in His own body on the cross, just as He bore his sin there, then he may have trouble receiving his healing. There are undoubtedly some in the body of Christ who are sick simply because they do not realize all that Christ's bodily suffering and death actually accomplished for them. Indeed, some Christians may have even perished simply because they lacked this knowledge.

Indeed, Moses, Isaiah, David, Solomon, Micah, Malachi, Matthew, James, Peter, Paul and Jesus are all witnesses that there is a definite, and very close, connection between sin and sickness, and between repentance and physical healing. That is because the atonement of Christ covers both mankind's sin and his sickness.

Jesus said that it was just as easy for Him to say, *"Thy sins be forgiven thee"* as it was for Him to say, *"be healed."* That is because He is both Savior of the soul and Healer of the body. The plan of God was, and is, that the salvation of souls should result in the healing of their bodies, whether immediate or gradual.

The late healing evangelist, Kathryn Kuhlman writes:

> "When Jesus died on the cross and cried out, 'it is finished!' He not only died for our sins but our sicknesses too. It took several months for me to realize that, for I had not been taught that there was healing for the body in the redemption of Christ. But then I read in Isaiah' where He was wounded for our transgressions, bruised for our iniquities, and by His stripes we are healed.' I had no choice but to accept that Jesus did not die just to open the way to heaven, but to provide healing as well." (p. 102)

Then she adds:

> "I knew that if I lived and died and never
> saw a single healing miracle like the apostles
> experienced in the book of Acts, it would not
> change God's word." (p. 102)

Miss Kulhman believed that healing was in the atonement, not because of the healings that she witnessed but
simply because she saw that truth in God's word.

John G. Lake was another well-known healing evangelist, who lived from 1870 - 1935 and saw multitudes saved
and healed as a result of his ministry in Africa, Canada and
in the United States. In the collection of his works, *John G
Lake: His Life, His Sermons, His Boldness of Faith,* it is
clear that he believed that when Christ comes into one's life,
healing begins in that one's spirit and works outward from
spirit to soul to body. (p. 3-14) He believed it so strongly and
preached it so convincingly that in Spokane, Washington
alone, where his headquarters were and where he established
"healing rooms," there were over 100,000 healings documented and reported in just five years. In the early 1920's, a
report out of Washington D.C. said that Rev. Lake, through
divine healing, has made Spokane, Washington the healthiest

city in the world, according to U. S. statistics. (p. xxx)

Many others with healing ministries in the past, such as Raymond T. Richey, A. B. Simpson, Dr. Charles Price, Andrew Murray, Aimee Semple McPherson, Oral Roberts, T.L. Osborn, Johann Blumhardt, A. J. Gordon, A. W. Tozer, Ethan Allen, Carrie Judd Montgomery, Maria Woodworth-Etter, F.F. Bosworth, Smith Wigglesworth and others, all believed and taught that healing was provided for in Christ's atonement. The results of their faith are well documented.

Many of these giants of faith were ridiculed, falsely accused, even thrown into jail, and the worst thing about their trials is that much of the opposition to their ministries came from the established Church. (Sounds like something right out of the New Testament, does it not?)

It is an interesting fact, and worthy of note, that those who believe that healing is in the atonement have witnessed many (some hundreds or thousands), healings take place under their ministries while those who do not believe it see few, if any, in their own ministries.

When the present day Church becomes convinced that God's word teaches healing in the atonement and that God's word is true regardless of the ability and desire of men to take hold of it, the Church will see God's healing power manifested in a much greater measure in its midst.

Chapter Four

The Promise of Long Life

God has not only promised and provided healing for His children when it is needed but He has purposed for them to live long and useful lives. Of course, the longevity He has promised is conditional, as are His healing promises.

The first condition is found in Exodus 20:12 and then reaffirmed in Eph. 6:1-3. The fifth commandment God gave to the children of Israel is the only commandment that contained a promise, and that promise is for long life:

> *"Honor your father and mother, **that your days may be long** upon the land which the Lord your God is giving you."*

The next condition is found in Exodus 23:20-26. There God tells His people that He is going to send an angelic messenger (a type of the Holy Spirit) before them to bring them into the land He has prepared for them. If they will listen to that messenger's voice and obey it, He will give them victory over their enemies, take sickness away from them, and - *"fulfill the number of their days"* (verse 26). In other words, they will not die prematurely, as some do that live or wander outside of God's protection. (Solomon wrote, in Ecclesiastes 7:17 that the overly wicked and foolish are in danger of dying before their time).

After Jesus' ascension into heaven, He sent his Holy Spirit to lead and guide His people into the promised blessings of God. Those who follow and obey Him consistently will see these promises fulfilled in their lives:

> *"That you may love the Lord your God, that you may obey His voice, and that you may cling to Him for He is your **life and the length of your days...**"* Deut. 30:20

> *"Because he has set his love upon Me.....**with long life I will satisfy him** and show him My salvation."* Ps. 91:14-16

> *"My son, do not forget My law, but let your heart keep My commands, for **length of days***

and long life *and peace will they add to you." —* Pro. 3:2

"Do not be wise in your own eyes. Fear the Lord and depart from evil. It will be **health to your flesh and strength to your bones."** *— Pro.3:7-8*

"My son, give attention to my words; incline your ears to My sayings. Do not let them depart from your eyes: keep them in the midst of your heart; for **they are life to those that find them and health to all their flesh."** — Pr. 4:20-22

"Hear My son and receive My sayings, **and the years of your life shall be many."** — Pro. 4:10

"For by me your **days will be multiplied and years of life will be added to you."** — Pro. 9:11

"The fear of the Lord **leads to life..."** — Pro. 19:23

However, to those who do not choose to obey Him, God says,

> *"The fear of the Lord prolongs days but the years of the wicked will be shortened."*
> —Pro. 10:27

> *"Your life shall hang in doubt before you. You shall fear day and night and* **have no assurance of life."**—Deut. 28:66

The apostle Peter gives some advice to those who would live long and fruitful days:

> "Foe h*e who would love life and see good days, let him refrain his tongue from evil, and his lips from speaking deceit, let him turn away from evil and do good, let him seek peace and pursue it" (I Peter 3:10, 11)*.

A. B. Simpson, the founder of the Christian and Missionary Alliance and a strong defender of the gospel of healing, addresses the question on whether the belief that God always wants to heal believers when they are sick might lead some to suppose that a Christian should never die:

"... why should faith go farther than the Word? Anything beyond that is presumption. The Word places a limit to human life, [Hebrews 9:27]and all that scriptural faith can claim is sufficiency of health and strength for our life-work and within its fair limits. It may be longer or shorter, but it need not, like the wicked, fail to live out half its days. It should be complete, satisfying, and as long as the work of life is yet undone. And then, when the close comes, why need it be with painful and depressing sickness, as the rotten apple falls in June from disease and with a worm at the root? Why may it not be rather as that ripe apple would drop in September, mature, mellow, and ready to fall without a struggle into the gardener's hand? So Job pictures the close of a good man's life as the full maturity of 'the shock of corn that cometh in its season [Job 5:26].'" (p.37)

Of course, God expects us to take care of our bodies and use them for His glory if we would experience long, satisfying and fruitful lives.

The Bible says, in I Cor. 6:13:

> *Now the body...is for the Lord and the Lord*
> *for the body.*

Verses 19 and 20 of the same chapter read:

> *"Or do you not know that your body is the*
> *temple of the Holy Spirit who is in you, whom*
> *you have from God and you are not your own?*
> *For you were bought with a price; therefore*
> *glorify God in your body and in your spirit,*
> *which are God's."*

Andrew Murray, well-known and much-loved Scottish preacher and Christian writer of the late nineteenth and early twentieth century, in his book, *"Divine Healing,"* writes:

> "In the same way in which the Holy Spirit
> brings to our soul and spirit the life of
> Jesus—His holiness, His joy, His strength—
> He comes also to impart to the sick body all
> the vigorous vitality of Christ as soon as the
> hand of faith is stretched out to receive it.

When the body is fully subjected to Christ, crucified with Him, renouncing all self-will and independence, desiring nothing but to be the Lord's temple, it is then that the Holy Spirit manifests the power of the risen Savior in the body..." (p. 42)

Mr. Murray states further:

"For the believer who has walked with his Savior, full of the strength that comes from divine healing, and under the influence of the Holy Spirit, it is not necessary that when it comes his time to die, he should die of sickness. The death of the believer, when the end of life has come, is to fall asleep in Jesus Christ (I Cor. 15:18). For him death is only sleep after fatigue, the entering into rest." (p. 61)

There is a wonderful and exciting promise given to those saints of God who are in, or about to enter, their senior years. It is found in Psalms 92:13:14:

*"Those who are planted in the house of the Lord shall flourish in the courts of our God. **They shall still bear fruit in old age:** they shall be fresh and flourishing."*

The word *"flourish"* according to the Random House Dictionary, means *"to be or to grow at a vigorous state. To be at the height of fame, excellence, and influence."* The American Heritage Dictionary says that *"flourish"* means *"to grow well or luxuriously: thrive"* or *"to do or fare well: succeed."*

In light of the previous scriptures, one wonders why there are so many present-day Christians suffering chronic, even debilitating diseases, that limit both their ministries and influence (or prohibit them altogether), and bring not only great physical and emotional distress to their families, but financial hardship as well.

Why are so many of God's older saints wasting away with cancer or Alzheimer's, or crippling arthritis, etc. and enjoying no quality of life at all? Are these promises of healing and long productive lives not for the Body of Christ? If they are, why are Christians not taking hold of them?

Chapter Five

The Fading of the Healing Ministry

Ⅰf healing was provided for God's people in the atonement of Christ, and God wants His people to live long and productive lives, why are God's people not experiencing the same? Why are Christians not being taught the truth about healing in many churches? Should all the blame be laid on present-day teachers and preachers for keeping believers in the dark or does the root of their failure to discern and teach the truth lie elsewhere?

An in-depth study of the history of Christianity will provide some answers to these questions and those who teach and preach the word of God need to give this history some serious study and thought. When they do, it should become evident that the ministry of healing and other manifestations of God's power ceased to exist in a large part of the established Church, not when the Apostles died, as many teach, but as sin and heresy crept in.

It was undoubtedly easier for those who had lived and walked with Jesus, saw His miracles, heard His teachings and who had been eye-witnesses to His resurrection, to hold fast to their faith and righteousness than it was for those who did not have this first-hand knowledge of Jesus. The apostles foresaw that with their death, and without their constant encouragement and watchful eyes, many in the Church would fall into deception and lethargy. They therefore warned the young Church to be steadfast and diligent and to encourage one another.

The apostles also foretold of the false prophets that would infiltrate the Church to turn many away from the faith. They warned that these prophets would teach both man-made doctrines and doctrines of demons (I Tim. 4:1-3). The scriptures show that this had begun to happen to some degree even while the Apostles were still alive (Gal. 3:1-3). Yet the greater manifestation of this prophecy happened over a period of a few hundred years as ungodly and power-hungry men began to assume headship of the Church. They put forth their own edicts and commandments, most of which were designed to keep their members under control while achieving for themselves fame and monetary gain.

In the early part of the fourth century, when the Emperor

Constantine made a profession of Christianity that ended the persecutions of Christians and made Christianity the state religion, many reprobates, pagans and other unbelievers inundated the Church. (It seems it takes persecution to keep the Church pure and free of those who are not totally dedicated to Christ.)

Their motive, it can be easily detected, was not to follow Christ, the God-ordained head of the Church, but to gain favor with the emperor. Of course, they brought their unscriptural, even pagan, beliefs and practices with them and, over time, these things were incorporated into the rituals and doctrines of the Church. (Sadly, many of them are still tolerated in some churches today).

When man became head of the Church, his word began to take precedence over the pure word of God. Eventually, even in so-called Christian churches, laymen were forbidden to read the Bible. Later, it became a crime, sometimes punishable by death, for anyone even to possess the word of God.

During this great falling-away period (II Thess. 2:3), the Holy Spirit's power and manifest presence was gradually withdrawn from the greater part of the organized Church. God will not share His glory with man, or His headship. Neither will He manifest His power through sin-filled vessels. With the Holy Spirit's withdrawal from a large portion of the Church, the spiritual gifts that are manifestations of His presence, such as healings, miracles, tongues, interpretations, etc. (I Corinthians 12: 7-10), gradually faded from the scene also.

Only in that sense can one say that healing, or any other supernatural manifestation of God's presence, ceased within the Church *after* (not *when or because*) the apostles died and it was certainly not God's plan according to Paul's first letter to the Corinthians.

The Church at Corinth was blessed to have the gifts of the Holy Spirit operating in their midst but they did not understand the purpose of the gifts so they were not functioning in them properly. Therefore, Paul instructs them in the use of the gifts after telling them that they should expect those gifts to be manifested in their midst until *Jesus returns to the earth.*

Here is how Paul's admonition in I Corinthians 1:7 reads in differing translations:

> *"So that you come behind in no gift; waiting for the coming of our Lord Jesus."* (NKJ)

> *"Therefore you do not lack any spiritual gift*

as you eagerly wait for our Lord Jesus Christ to be revealed." (NIV)

"Now you have every grace and blessing; every spiritual gift and power for doing His will are yours during this time of waiting for the return of our Lord Jesus Christ." (LB)

"So that you are not lacking in any gift, as you wait for the revealing of our Lord Jesus Christ." (RSV)

Paul's statement here gives a better understanding of what he meant in I Cor. 13: 8-10. He says there that certain spiritual gifts will pass away when *"that which is perfect"* comes. Because he also says that all the spiritual gifts are to be present in the Church until Jesus comes back, *"that which is perfect"* can only mean the Lord Jesus Himself, not His written word, as some suppose.

When the manifestations of the Holy Spirit became less frequent in a large part of the established Church, Satan saw his opportunity to deceive God's people for generations to come. Satan is a master at brainwashing—he invented it! His methods are to present half-truths as whole truths, to misinterpret truth, or to blind people from the truth. Now there are pastors who truly believe, and understandably so, that the reason they do not see the supernatural manifestations of God's presence and power (and this includes healings) in their churches and lives is because they ceased operating when the original twelve apostles died. What other explanation can there be?

While Jesus and the apostles warned the new Church that after they were gone all hell would come against the Church, Jesus promised hell would not prevail — and it has not! God has always had His remnant!

There have always been those comparatively few individuals who have held fast to the word of God and to righteousness and have travailed in prayer for a wayward Church. The Reformation began with Martin Luther's protest against false doctrine and ungodly practices in the man-made and man-run Church in the 1600s. That Reformation has evolved into the *Restoration* that has been taking place in the Church throughout the last two hundred years or so. God has been restoring the ministry of the spiritual gifts, including healing, to the Church as His faithful remnant has earnestly sought cleansing and restoration for the body of Christ.

That is as it should be. Christians preach that they serve a risen Savior, One who is still involved in the affairs of mankind. How is the world to know this if His power is no longer demonstrated through His Church? The living Lord is coming back for a victorious Church—an overcoming Church—not one that is sick, weak and powerless, *"having a form of godliness but denying its power..."* (II Tim. 3:5).

When Jesus sent the twelve, and later the seventy, out to preach the gospel, He commanded them to heal the sick and cast out devils. He said in Mark 16: 15-18 that *those who believe* would lay hands on the sick and they *would* recover. The Bible clearly teaches that physical healing and deliverance from demons was to be an accompanying benefit and sign to those who would receive the gospel.

In every genuine move of God since Martin Luther's time, the Holy Spirit has manifested His presence and power, by not just a few, but multitudes being saved, healed and set free from some type of Satanic bondage. Not only have individual lives been changed, but entire cities have been changed as God has poured out His Spirit in those areas. For example, in the not too distant past, during the Welsh Revival of 1904-1905, *"Whole communities [had been] turned 'upside down* [see Acts 17:6],'" as a result of conviction by the Holy Spirit and by the repentance of the people. Bars and public houses (of prostitution) had been shut down as the owners and inhabitants were converted (Truth in

History, n.d., Effects of the revival, para. 1).

Yet many of those who call themselves God's people were, and are, the very ones who Satan has used, and *is* using, to try to quench these revival fires. Some of these people have truly not understood or recognized God's working in their midst while others are simply satisfied with the status quo. They have all of God that they want and prefer to hang onto their man-made traditions, rituals, doctrines, pet sins, political correctness, and friendship with the world, rather than let the Holy Spirit have full control of their lives and ministries.

Thank God that there are many churches today that are refusing to compromise the Word of God. Those churches are teaching, preaching and practicing the whole counsel of God and are seeing the Word confirmed with signs following. These have not all been classic Pentecostal groups either, as some people believe. Great revivals, with the manifestations of healing, deliverance and other spiritual gifts, have taken place among Lutherans, Presbyterians, Episcopalians, Catholics and other main-line denominations throughout the last two hundred years or more.

However, there is still a large portion of the Church that is resisting what God wants to do in their midst, even to the point of attributing the work of the Holy Spirit to Satan.

Although this is being done for the most part in ignorance, it is treading on very dangerous ground!

The fading of the healing ministry and ignorance of how that came about has fostered much erroneous thinking on the subject of healing. The following chapters will address some of those misconceptions in the light of God's word and other things that hinder one's ability to receive healing from God.

Part Two

Hindrances to Healing

Chapter Six

Paul's Thorn – II Corinthians 12:1-10

Many Christians believe that the apostle Paul had a chronic sickness that was given to him by God and that God refused to heal despite several pleas from Paul that He do so. Because of this common theory (and it *is* just a theory) about Paul's *"thorn"* being a chronic disease, many people believe that they too, have a "thorn" of sickness from which they cannot hope or expect to be healed. When you try to encourage them to believe God for healing, they will say, *"But what about Paul's thorn? If God wouldn't heal such a faithful [full-of-faith] servant as Paul, how can I expect Him to heal me?"*

Among those who believe this theory, there is much speculation and disagreement about what Paul's disease might have been. Some feel that Paul had malaria. Others suppose it was epilepsy, migraines, a stuttering tongue, bad eyesight, an eye disease, blindness or even leprosy.

Most of these people cannot give any scriptural evidence for believing as they do, they are just quoting what they have heard others say. Those that do try to present scriptural evidence for the *"Paul's thorn-in-the-flesh was a chronic disease"* theory have three main scriptures that they feel best supports their view. Those scriptures are II Corinthians 12:1-10, Galatians 4:13-15 and II Corinthians 10:10.

Because so many people stumble over what they believe to be Paul's thorn, it would be appropriate to examine the three scriptures above in light of *all* that Paul has to say about his life and ministry and God's dealings with him.

II Corinthians 12:1-10

In the first six verses of this passage of scripture, Paul talks about an experience he has had where he was *"caught up to the third heaven"* and heard and saw such extraordinary things that he was forbidden by God to share them with his readers. Then he says, in verses 7-10,

> *"and lest I be exalted above measure, by the abundance of revelations, **a thorn in the flesh was given unto me, a messenger of Satan** to*

buffet me, lest I be exalted above measure. Concerning this thing, I pleaded with the Lord three times that it might depart from me. And He said to me, 'My grace is sufficient for you. For My strength is made perfect in weakness.' Therefore most gladly will I boast in my infirmities, that the power of Christ may rest upon me. Therefore I take pleasure in infirmities, in reproaches, in needs, in persecutions, in distresses, for Christ's sake. For when I am weak, I am strong."

Notice that Paul does not say here, or even imply, that his thorn was a sickness. He does tell us exactly what it was. He says, quite clearly, in verse 7, that his *"thorn"* was *"a messenger of Satan."* He says it was a *personality*—a *demonic being*. Paul does not even say that the Lord refused to *heal* him. He says that he asked the Lord three times to *remove* the *"thorn"* (the demonic being) and that the Lord told Paul that His grace would be sufficient for any *weakness* that Paul would experience.

There is no indication in these verses that Paul had a chronic disease that was God's will for his life and therefore God refused to heal him of that particular disease. Yet many people who believe otherwise will base their belief on this passage of scripture alone and they are simply reading into the word of God something that is not there. Perhaps it is because they can find no other explanation for the meaning of this passage.

What did Paul mean by saying that the messenger of Satan was a *"thorn in the flesh?"* To understand that one needs to look at how that expression might be used elsewhere in God's word. Actually, the exact expression *"thorn in the flesh"* is not used anywhere else in God's word but Numbers 33:55 reads:

> **"But** *if you do not drive out the inhabitants of the land from before you, then it shall be that those whom you let remain shall be irritants in your eyes and **thorns in your sides,** and they shall harass you in the land where you dwell."*

Judges 2:3 reads:

> *"Therefore I also said that I would not drive them out before you; but they shall be **thorns in your side**, and their gods shall be a snare to you."*

Joshua 23:13 speaks of *thorns in your eyes*:

> *"Know for certain that the Lord your God will no longer drive out those nations from before you. But they shall be snares and traps to you, and scourges on your sides and **thorns in your eyes**, until you perish from the good land which the Lord your God has given you."*

In each of these scriptures, the phrases containing the word *"thorn"* are clearly used metaphorically and refers to *people* that would become a source of harassment to the children of Israel if the Israelites made alliances with them instead of overcoming them.

In the same metaphorical way, Paul was using the expression *"thorn in the flesh"* to describe the harassment of Satan in his own life, which God was allowing to keep Paul from becoming *"exalted above measure."* In other words, to keep him humble and dependent upon God.

Paul says the messenger was in his life to *buffet* him (II Cor. 12:7). The word *"buffet"* is the Greek word *"kolaphizo"* and means *"to strike with the hands and fist"* according to Vine's Complete Expository Dictionary. (p. 82) The Jewish

New Testament translates II Cor. 12:7 this way:

*"Therefore to keep me from becoming overly proud, I was given a thorn In my flesh to **pound away at me** [buffet] that I wouldn't grow conceited."*

Paul was using the word *"buffet"* metaphorically also because, although Paul received numerous beatings from the hands of people that Satan stirred up against him, he was attacked in many other ways as well.

What Paul was actually talking about in this passage was the spiritual warfare that he found himself engaged in as soon as he became a follower and preacher of Christ. That warfare evidently increased in intensity as his knowledge of God and his influence grew. The Bible clearly teaches that every believer who does anything at all to advance the spread of the gospel will find themselves attacked, or *"buffeted"* in various ways by Satan's messengers who seek to hinder the word and the work of God from going forward. (Paul has much to say on the subject of spiritual warfare in his letters to the early Church, which will be examined further in chapter eleven. Of course, if one has not been taught to expect spiritual warfare as a part of his spiritual experience, it will be easy for them to overlook what Paul actually said his thorn was or to look for some hidden meaning).

Paul no doubt experienced more intense warfare than most Christians ever will. He was probably the greatest apostle of them all, as men count greatness. His missionary journeys resulted in the initial spread of the gospel to the Gentiles and to many nations. His letters containing the revelation of God to him have been a comfort, strength, guide, and encouragement to countless individuals through the ages.

It is certain that while every true Christian will at times experience the attacks of Satan upon his life and ministry in some degree, Paul's unique role in the forming and strengthening of the Church and his understanding of spiritual things made him a primary target of Satanic forces.

It is highly possible that Paul's petitioning of the Lord to remove his thorn in the flesh was an expression of his weariness of the constant attacks of Satan upon his life. Perhaps he felt that he could get a lot more accomplished for God and accomplish it quicker if God would just smooth out the path for him a little—for instance, allow him to defeat Satan all at once, instead of battle by battle.

Every Christian who is truly committed to fulfilling God's will for his life will find the going hard at times and perhaps even be tempted to drop out of the race. Considering all the persecution Paul went through it is not hard to believe that he, too, had his moments of despair. After all, he is the one to whom God revealed the truth that one must not be "weary in well doing, for in due season we shall reap, if we do not lose heart" (Galatians 6:9).

Paul's cry for deliverance from the messenger of Satan was similar to Jesus' cry in the garden of Gethsemene when, in His humanity, He felt that His own cross was too heavy to bear (Luke 22:42). God did not remove the cup of suffering from Jesus either but gave Him added strength and grace to bear it.

Although Christians have been given both the power and the responsibility to overcome their enemy when he comes against them, they do not have the authority to prevent his attacks. God allowed Job to be tested by Satan, His own Son to be tested by Satan and He allows all true Christians to be tested by Satan as well.

Satan is not as powerful as God is, but he is more powerful than Christians are in their humanity. Satan's buffetings in the Christian's life serve to remind him how impotent he is in his own strength and how much he needs to rely upon God's strength to live the Christian life and to do what God has called him to do.

Satan's attacks (*"fiery darts"* see Ephesians 6:16) on Paul took many forms and they will in the Christian's life, also. Just when one thinks he has gotten wise to Satan's tactics in one area and has learned to resist him there, he will attack in an entirely different area and fashion. Paul lists some of the different ways in which he was attacked (buffeted) by Satan in II Corinthians 11:23-28:

"I am in labors more abundant, in stripes above measure, in prisons more frequently, in deaths often. From the Jews five times I received forty stripes minus one. Three times I was beaten with rods, once I was stoned: three times I was shipwrecked, a night and a day I have been in the deep; in journeys often, in perils of waters, in perils of robbers, in perils of my own countrymen, in perils of the Gentiles, in perils in the city, in perils in the wilderness, in perils in the sea, in perils among false brethren: in weariness and toil, in sleeplessness often, in hunger and thirst, in fastings often, in cold and nakedness— besides the other things that come upon me daily: my deep concern for all the churches."

Notice that Paul does not list sickness here or anywhere else as one of the trials he suffered. It does seem that if Paul had a chronic sickness that plagued him so much that he asked the Lord three times to remove it, he would have included, *"in sickness often"* in this list of trials but he did not.

The fact is, there is no clear evidence that Paul was troubled with a chronic disease—*"chronic"* meaning *"over a long time, of long standing, recurring frequently"* according to The Random House Dictionary. (Chronic disease is, no doubt, what is meant by *"prolonged sicknesses"* in Duet. 28:59, from which God promised to spare those that were obedient to Him).

Was Paul *ever* sick? No one really knows. He most likely had some common maladies from time to time, (as most people do) but if so, they were evidently not serious enough or prolonged enough for him to consider them worth mentioning. The only Biblical record of Satan's *attempt* to inflict Paul with sickness, or death by sickness, is the one in which Satan failed miserably because Paul, being submitted to God (James 4:7), resisted his enemy's attack and overcame him. The account of that event can be found in Acts 28:3-9:

> *"But when Paul had gathered a bunch of sticks and laid them on the fire, a viper came out of the heat and fastened on his hand. So*

when the natives saw the creature hanging from his hand, they said to one another, 'No doubt this man is a murderer, whom, though he has escaped from the sea, yet justice does not allow to live.' But he shook off the creature into the fire and suffered no harm. However, they were expecting that he would swell up or suddenly fall down dead. But after they had looked for a long time and saw no harm come to him, they changed their mind and said that he was a god. In that region there was an estate of a leading citizen of the island, whose name was Publius, who received us and entertained us courteously for three days. And it happened that the father of Publius lay sick of a fever and dysentery. Paul went into him and prayed and he laid his hands on him and healed him. So when this was done, the rest of those on the island who had diseases also came and were healed."

Considering the fact that more people were ministered to and healed than would have been had the attack of the viper not occurred, one can understand why God allowed it!

Obviously, it was Paul's *victory* over the poisonous snake that inspired the natives to come to Paul for healing.

Everywhere Paul went, as he preached the gospel, God confirmed His word with signs following, as He promised. Paul not only preached the healing/delivering power of God as part of the gospel message, but he practiced it as well. The Bible says, in Acts 19:11-12:

"God wrought special miracles by the hand of Paul so that even handkerchiefs or aprons were brought from his body to the sick, and the diseases left them and the evil spirits went out of them."

It seems likely that if Paul himself had been denied healing from God of a chronic disease—particularly one that was highly visible, as many suppose, it would have been difficult for him to have faith for the healing of others or for those others to believe that the power of God would flow through Paul to meet their need.

Chapter Seven

Paul's Thorn -
Galatians 4:13-15

T his scripture also has caused some people to conclude that Paul had a chronic disease that God refused to heal. However, if one carefully studies this passage of scripture along with other statements that Paul made about himself, one has to realize that there is more than one interpretation that can be made of it and perhaps even one that is more compatible with other scriptures as well. Galatians 4:13-15 reads:

> *"You know that because of physical infirmity*
> *I preached the gospel to you at first. And my*
> *trial which was in my flesh, you did not despise*
> *or reject, but you received me as an angel of*
> *God, even as Christ Jesus. What then was the*
> *blessing you enjoyed? For I bear you witness*
> *that, if possible, you would have plucked out*

your own eyes and given them to me."

It is understandable that many Christians conclude from this scripture that Paul is saying his *"trial which was in my flesh"* was a chronic disease. However, there are several reasons why this conclusion is not the only one that can be made.

To begin with, the word *"infirmity"* as used here, and in all other scriptures except one means *"weakness"*, not *"sickness"*, according to Vines' Complete Expository Dictionary. (p. 324) The exception is in Luke 7:21 where the word *"infirmity"* is translated in the King James Version as *"diseases"* but the original Greek word used there is a different word than the one used in Paul's writings.

So the use of the phrase *"physical infirmity"* does not necessarily mean that Paul had a disease but rather a physical weakness that others could readily detect and for which they might despise or reject Paul.

Some feel that the statement Paul made, *"For I bear you witness, that if possible, you would have plucked out your own eyes and given them to me."* is proof that Paul had one of these three conditions:

Chronic poor eyesight

Blindness

A chronic Oriental eye disease

It is hard to make a solid case for any of those conditions in light of other scriptures that reveal certain things about Paul. Poor eyesight by itself seems hardly a valid reason for people to despise or reject Paul. Paul certainly was not blind, because it is known that he wrote many of his letters to the churches by his own hand. When Paul met Jesus on the road to Damascus, Paul was stricken blind for three days after which God healed his sight through the ministry of Ananias (Acts 9:1-18).

Some believers mistakenly believe that God struck Paul with blindness, but Paul himself says in Acts 22:11 that it was for *"the glory of the light"* that he could not see. In other words, the sight of the glorified Christ was too much for Paul's natural eyes to endure. God did restore Paul's sight three days later, and it does not do justice to God, whose gifts and callings are irrevocable (Romans 11:29), to suppose that he would later take back His gift of healing to leave Paul partially blind the rest of his life, or to suppose that he would leave him with a repulsive eye disease.

What did Paul mean then by saying,

"For I bear you witness that, if possible, you would have plucked out your own eyes and given them to me." (Gal. 4:15)?

The Wycliffe Bible Commentary on the New Testament states that the phrase, *"ye would have plucked out your own eyes and given them to me"* is not necessarily proof that the apostle had eye trouble. (p. 710) The eyes are probably singled out for their preciousness."

T.L. Osborn Sr., well-known evangelist of the last century, relates an interesting occurrence in his book, *"Healing the Sick."* He tells about an evangelistic campaign that he held in Jamaica for thirteen weeks during which many people were saved and many were miraculously healed. When he was preparing to leave that country, one of the local pastors came to him and said:

"Brother Osborn, our people love you. They are thankful to God for your coming to us and they want you to know that they would cut off their right arm and give it to you if it were possible." (p. 175)

Rev. Osborn then stated that their statement did not mean that there was something wrong with his arm, because there was not. The statement was obviously a metaphorical one intended to express the tremendous gratitude of the Jamaican people for Rev. Osborn's ministry to them.

So the Galatians remark about giving their own eyes to Paul does not necessarily mean that Paul had some on-going abnormal eye condition. However, it is quite likely that there was actually something wrong with Paul's eyes *at the time of which he was speaking*.

The New International Version of the Bible suggests that the "*physical infirmity*" that Paul was speaking of could have been bruises, a broken bone, swelling or distortion of the face due to some recent beating or stoning that Paul had experienced. Paul may have had, among other things, "*black*" and swollen eyes.

All of these things—bruises, broken bones, swelling and distortion of the face or body caused from a beating or a stoning—would have been temporary, though certainly unsightly, and in the case of a broken bone, temporarily disabling.

Of whatever physical infirmity Paul was speaking, he does imply that it was temporary. He says in verse 13 that the infirmity was present when he *first* preached the gospel to them, and he called it a trial. (A trial, in the Biblical sense, is a temporary discomfort that God allows one to go through in order to work His purpose in that one's life and that one can expect it to end when that purpose is accomplished).

On Paul's first visit to preach the gospel in Asia, he was stoned so badly in Lystra, that he was left for dead (Acts 14:8-21). Yet the Lord revived him and *the very next day,* he preached the gospel in Derby, then he went on to preach again in Lystra, Iconium and Antioch—all cities of Galatia. Paul may very well have still had some of the physical scars from this stoning when he preached in some of those cities.

Perhaps Paul's bruised and battered body gave him the appearance of a street fighter rather than a messenger of the gospel of love, peace and healing. Perhaps that's what he meant by saying that the people did not *"despise or reject"* him because of his *"flesh."*

Referring to his near death experience in Asia, Paul said he would have died if it had not been for his trust in the One who could raise the dead. This is what he wrote to the Corinthians:

"For we do not want you to be ignorant, Brethren, of our trouble which came to us in Asia; that we were burdened beyond measure, above strength, so that we despaired even of life. Yes, we had the sentence of death in ourselves, that we should not trust in ourselves but in God Who raises the dead,

> *Who **delivered** us from so great a death, and*
> ***does deliver** us: in whom we trust that He **will***
> ***still** deliver us."* (II Cor. 1:8-10).

After the stoning in Lystra, and perhaps because of it, Paul's expectation was *always* that God would deliver him, by His grace, from whatever came against him as he carried out the will of God for his life.

In the book of Timothy, written shortly before Paul's death, *after* he had written about his troubles in Asia and elsewhere, and *after* he had written about his thorn, Paul makes another great declaration:

> *"Persecutions, afflictions which happened to*
> *me at Antioch, at Iconium, at Lystra, what*
> *persecutions I endured. And out of them **all***
> *the Lord delivered me"* (II Tim. 3:11).

According to Vines Complete Expository Dictionary (New Testament words), the Greek words for "affliction" are never translated "sickness"either, but rather as ill treatment, anguish, distress, persecution, torment, suffering, etc. (p. 17) Certainly, sickness can be a source of misery, torment, suffering and distress, but where it is not translated that way in the scripture, we cannot say that is what Paul meant.

James makes a very clear distinction between "affliction" and "sickness" in chapter five of his gospel when he instructs those who are *afflicted* to pray and those who are *sick* to call for the elders of the church to anoint him with oil and pray for him. *However, if Paul had been talking about sickness in this passage, he would also be claiming that the Lord had delivered him of it!*

In II Corinthians 12:9, Paul says that Jesus told him that His grace was sufficient for Paul and that His strength is made perfect in weakness. Notice, Jesus did not say that His strength was made perfect in *sickness* but in *weakness*. There is really no indication that Jesus was talking about sickness here at all, but there is much evidence elsewhere in the scripture to suggest that He was simply talking about man's limitations and inadequacies.

Paul goes on to say, in verses 9 and 10:

> *Therefore will I boast in my infirmities (weaknesses) that the power of Christ may rest upon me. Therefore I take pleasure in infirmities (weaknesses), in reproaches, in needs, in persecutions, in distresses for Christ's sake. For*

when I am weak, then I am strong.

There is no mention of sickness in this passage, either. Paul does not say that he takes pleasure in *sickness*, but in *weakness*.

What were some of Paul's weaknesses? No one knows them all, of course, but II Cor. 12:7 suggests that being lifted up with pride was both a possibility and a danger in Paul's life. In the next chapter, Paul himself mentions a weakness that he seemed to be acutely aware of and for which he felt he needed God's grace and power.

Chapter Eight

Paul's Thorn -
II Corinthians 10:10

This is the third scripture that people sometimes use as evidence that Paul had a permanent physical disability. The scripture reads:

> *"For his letters, they say, are weighty and powerful, but his bodily presence is weak, and his speech contemptible."*

Some people take Paul's words here to mean that Paul was of slight build or deformed or disfigured in some way. Others feel that he stuttered or had some kind of speech impediment.

These things could be true, of course, but to conclude that from what Paul actually said is pure conjecture, as the scripture is vague about what Paul meant by *"weak bodily presence"* and *"contemptible"* speech. It is quite possible that this scripture has nothing to do with a physical abnormality or affliction.

Paul is speaking here of how he thinks other people perceived him. Whether he was right about that or not, Paul evidently judged himself a poor speaker. For one who has been called to preach, that can be a painful shortcoming! Paul was a highly educated man (like Moses) but, as he tells us, he was *"...untrained in speech..."* (II Cor. 11:6). Here is how he is quoted in different translations:

KJV — *"though I be rude in speech, yet not in knowledge."*

NIV — *"I may not be a trained speaker, but I do have knowledge."*

RSV — *"Even if I am unskilled in speaking, I am not in knowledge."*

The Living Bible paraphrase:

> *"If I am a poor speaker, at least I know what I am talking about."*

Paul also writes, in I Cor. 2:1-5:

*"And I, brethren, when I came to you, did not come with **excellence of speech or of wisdom** declaring to you the testimony of God. For I was determined not to know anything among you except Jesus Christ and Him crucified. **I was with you in weakness, in fear, and in much trembling. And my speech and my preaching were not with persuasive words of human wisdom,** but in the demonstration of the Spirit and of power, that your faith should not stand in the wisdom of men but in the power of God."*

Paul seemed to believe that there was a marked difference between his oral presentations of the gospel and his written ones. His letters, he felt, had the greater impact on people. It is hard for believers who have only his letters to imagine that Paul may have been shy or self-conscious about speaking in person. For others, Paul's self-evaluation is not so hard to understand. Many writers and poets have said that they are not able to stand before a crowd and speak nearly as fluently or eloquently as they can with a pen in their hand.

Shyness and/or self-consciousness, as well as a lack of oratory skills, can greatly reduce the effectiveness of a speaker's message. (Moses, too, was undoubtedly a highly educated man but he also felt that he was lacking in communication skills—Exodus 4:10). God's solution for both men was that God would work through them in acts of great power to prove that they had been sent and anointed of God.

Considering II Cor. 10:10, in light of everything that Paul has to say about himself, one must realize that there is another possible interpretation of what Paul meant here than that which is usually given. That is that Paul simply felt that he lacked the personal charisma, social graces, and eloquent speech that draws the attention of others and makes one an interesting, popular and convincing speaker!

Since Paul had no great oratorical skills or personal magnetism with which to persuade men to follow Christ, he had to rely on the power of God being manifested through him to capture and hold his audience's attention long enough to persuade them to embrace Christianity.

Paul was acutely aware of his own weaknesses and shortcomings, as all Christian ought to be. Were it not for the grace of God being constantly applied to Christians' life, none of them would be fit for His service. If God did not allow Satan to buffet believers they might neglect to stay close to Him and constantly seek His strength and His presence. Easy victories, unique experiences, or abundant revelations might cause individuals to think they were something or somebody in themselves and thus rob God of His glory.

Paul knew that he had a special calling from God (although it is doubtful that he knew the way his letters would be used) and he knew that he had been given unusual experiences and revelations from God. He also knew, from the constant buffeting of Satan in his life, that he was nothing and could do nothing, apart from the grace and power of God.

So, one must realize, on careful examination of scripture, that the argument most often used to prove that Paul's thorn-in-the-flesh was a chronic disease that God refused to heal is very weak, if not non-existent. Moreover, it is incompatible with all else that the Apostle Paul wrote of himself and of God's dealings with him.

Why is it important that Christians understand that the theory that Paul had a chronic disease, which God refused to heal, is just that—a theory, not an established fact?

Christians would probably be shocked by the number of individuals in the kingdom of God who have been deceived into accepting their chronic illness as a *"thorn in the flesh"* from God—because of a theory that has been taught as a fact—and because of this deception has been discouraged from both asking and expecting God to heal them. So they have resigned themselves to a lifetime of physical discomfort and limitation that is not God's will for them at all.

Many of these people do not stop to consider that even if Paul was allowed to suffer a chronic disease to keep him from being prideful, they need not fear a similar fate unless they, too, have received such abundant, extraordinary and unspeakable revelations as Paul, not to mention his high-calling and extensive influence.

Jesus did not come to kill or to make anyone sick. He said that He came to give mankind abundant life (John 10:10). A life plagued by chronic illness is hardly an abundant life. However, Christians have an enemy who does want to hinder or even kill them with sickness. Jesus warns in that same scripture that the thief comes to steal, kill and destroy.

God's promises of healing and deliverance are for all who will believe them and act upon them. God is no respecter of persons (Acts 10:34) but the enemy, Satan, would try to say that God is.

For several years after I became a Christian, I struggled with a cigarette habit. I knew that that habit was destroying my health. Also, I knew that God had the power to deliver me from both the habit and its damaging physical effects. As a result, I sought Him earnestly to do so.

One day Satan whispered in my ear that even though God had the power to deliver me and had done it for others that I knew, He was going to make an *exception* in my case because *"God wants to use you in a very special way."* God was going to make an example of me and let me die of lung cancer to help many others see the dangers of smoking and to inspire them to quit. Oh, I would go to heaven all right but I would just go there before most of my loved ones, including my small children.

I felt that this must be God speaking to me — I had told Him when I first became a Christian that I was willing to be used of Him in any way that He saw fit. However, instead of this word from *"God"* bringing hope, comfort and encouragement to me (James 3:17), it caused a great cloud of fear, sadness, and isolation to envelope me.

But, as I continued to study God's word under faithful teachers and preachers, I soon learned how to distinguish between the voice of God and that of the enemy of my soul and how to use the pure word of God against that enemy, Satan.

This incident happened over forty years ago. I have been free of the smoking habit and its damaging physical effects for all this time and God has used me in many ways to help build up the Body of Christ.

Any Christian who is suffering from chronic illness and who has given up hope of being healed simply because he believes his illness is a *"thorn in the flesh"* that God wills for to him to bear, should prayerfully and carefully study for himself what God's word has to say about sickness and healing and let God speak His truth to him.

Chapter Nine

Sin

A lthough sin is not the only cause of sickness being present in the life of a Christian, it is probably more often the cause than some would like to admit.

When Christians sin and do not quickly repent of that sin, they open a door to the enemy of their souls, Satan. The Bible says, *"Therefore submit to God. Resist the devil and he will flee from you"* (James 4:7). On the other hand, if one yields to Satan by resisting God, that individual gives Satan power in his life which means that Satan has permission to afflict that one in a variety of ways, not just sickness.. It is important to realize that the more one yields to Satan by failing to yield to God, the stronger hold Satan will have in one's life and the harder the battle might be to free one's self from his power. One must realize, of course, that no Christian is perfect. Every Christian has faults, weaknesses and failures that they grieve over and are continually seeking

God's help to overcome. As long as one sincerely desires to overcome those things, God will work in his life and eventually give him the victory.

However, some Christians knowingly allow sin to remain in their lives and refuse to seek God's help to overcome them because they enjoy their deceitful and/or momentary pleasures. Their sin may be a blatant violation of God's commandments or it may be a matter of sinful attitudes, such as the harboring of anger, unforgiveness, jealousy, resentment, revenge, bitterness, etc. Most physicians agree that these negative emotions can manifest themselves in sickness and disease. For instance, unforgiveness, hatred, resentment, desire for revenge, envy, etc., can cause arthritic symptoms.

Some years ago there was a young Christian lady named Jane who began to experience an aching in her bones, which worsened with time, keeping her awake at night and greatly slowing down her daytime activity.

Trips to the doctor who performed several tests, revealed no abnormalities. Pain medication helped some but sapped her strength and had other undesirable side effects.

Finally, Jane asked the elders of the church to anoint her with oil and pray for her healing. Before that took place, however, her pastor asked her to describe her discomfort. She had to think for a moment, then said, "*It's a little hard to describe what I feel, but my bones ache a lot in the daytime and when I lie still at night, my bones seem to creak and feel brittle as if they were about to disintegrate at any moment."*

Then the pastors and elders anointed Jane with oil and prayed for her. There was no immediate change in Jane's condition. but about a week later, she was invited to a home Bible study where the ladies there were studying what the Bible had to say about different emotions. Each week they chose a different emotion such as, anger, resentment, fear, worry, disappointment, grief, etc.

This particular week the Bible study focus was on jealousy. Jane felt that this subject could not apply to her and began to wish that she had not come. She started thinking about all the other things she could have been doing at home that day, and was hardly listening to what was being discussed at the time.

Suddenly her attention was caught by a Bible verse that was being read aloud. It was Proverbs 14:30:

"... envy is rottenness to the bones."

*"Why, that's **exactly** how my bones feel," she* thought, *"like they are rotten! But, surely, as a mature Christian, I am not guilty of such a petty thing as envy!"*

As the Bible study went on, the Jane began to experience a new kind of discomfort, this time not in her body, but in her spirit as the Lord began to show her what was in her heart that she had been refusing to look at and to acknowledge.

There was a lady in her church who *"annoyed"* her greatly. She was a tireless worker whom everyone admired and she had gifts and abilities that Jane did not have. Jane felt so intimidated and inadequate in the other lady's presence that lately she had been avoiding her as much as possible. Jane had even begun to criticize this lady even though others were extolling her virtues.

By the time the Bible study was over, Jane had realized that her physical discomfort was a symptom of a spiritual problem and God, by the light of His word, had diagnosed both her physical problem and her spiritual one.

Jane asked the other ladies to pray for her that day, not for her aching bones but that she would overcome her envy. In just a short time, as Jane began to work on her relationship with the lady she had envied, Jane's physical problem was completely gone. She and the other lady eventually became good friends.

Jane's story illustrates just one of the ways in which God's word brings healing to individuals. What happened to Jane is exactly what James was talking about when he said, *"Confess your trespasses* [faults] *to one another and pray for one another that you might be healed . . ."* (James 5:16). Sometimes people ask for healing when they should be confessing their sin; then the healing would come as they are cleansed from that sin.

What other clues does the Bible hold as to the cause of certain illnesses?

Eccl. 7:9 says,

> *"Do not be hasty in your spirit to be angry, for anger rests in the bosom* [chest, heart] *of fools."*

The medical profession tells us that anger, both that which is expressed in rage and that which is suppressed for a long period, can result in heart problems. That information was revealed in the Bible quite a long time before physicians discovered it.

It is important to consult God about sickness as well as seek medical help. There are no incurable or hard-to-diagnose diseases with God. Why do Christians let earthly doctors have the last or even the *only* word in our lives? Why do they not consult the Great Physician also, and see if there is something in their lives that is blocking His healing flow?

God's powerful word is an awesome diagnostic tool and remedy. Psalm 107 says that when the children of Israel sinned against God, *"He sent His word and healed them... from their destructions"* (verse 20). If sickness has a spiritual cause, The Holy Spirit and the word of God can get to the root of the problem and bring healing when doctors and medicine cannot.

If one simply takes medicine to alleviate the symptoms of what is a spiritual problem, and does not consult the Great Physician to see if the problem is spiritual, he will still have a spiritual problem and eventually his physical symptoms will worsen.

When one sins against God and refuses to acknowledge and forsake his sin, whether it be in word, deed or thought, he aligns himself with the wicked of this world. Psalm 50: 16-17 reads,

> *"But to the wicked God says: what right have you to declare My statues, or take my covenant in your mouth, seeing you hate instruction and cast my words behind you?"*

Christians can claim scripture and rebuke Satan all

day long, but if they are in willful disobedience to God or hanging on to a sinful attitude, this type of verbalizing will be to no avail.

Sometimes believers bring sickness on themselves by an over-indulgence of food, drink, medicine, work, play, etc. In this day of an abundance of fast, rich foods, extreme busyness and an increasing number of pleasures constantly calling for one's use and abuse, it is easy to overtax the body or neglect its needs. That is sin, because it is failing to take care of the body which God has given to mankind to glorify Himself.

I Cor. 3:16 - 17 reads:

> *"Do you not know that you are the temple of God, and that the Spirit of God dwells in you? If anyone destroys the temple of God, God will destroy him. For the temple of God is holy, which temple you are."*

Instead of eating, drinking, working, playing or medicating oneself in moderation and according to Biblical guidelines, Christians indulge their flesh as though it were God, and starve their spirit. Then they wonder why they are not healed.

The failure to take care of the body is the cause of many chronic diseases but, unfortunately, that is one thing many Christians are reluctant to do anything about. They would rather put up with their chronic disease than give up their overindulgence or their sinful pleasures. If one is not willing to give up whatever is hindering his healing, it is useless and even hypocritical to ask for prayer for healing. Christians should admit that their physical discomfort is their own fault and not God's.

I Cor. 11:29-32 says, that sickness and even premature death can come to believers as judgment for unconfessed sin in their lives. One cannot ignore the conviction of sin that the Holy Spirit brings, because it may result in their own destruction.

Proverbs 29:1 says,

> *"He who is often rebuked, and hardens his neck, will suddenly be destroyed and that without remedy."*

Occasionally, Christians say that sometimes they are destined to get sick just because they live in an imperfect, sinful world. Whether or not that is true, believers still cannot use living in an imperfect world as an excuse not to seek and believe God for healing any more than they can excuse their sinning because they live in a sinful world and not seek God for strength to overcome. Christians may live in this world but they are not of this world and they have something that the world does not have—a promise of healing.

The same God who is able to keep His children from falling into sin (Jude, verse 24) is not only able to heal them when they are sick, but is also able to protect them from sickness altogether. If the truth were known, much sickness comes, not because one lives in a sinful and fallen world, but because there is so much of the world in *him.*

It is foolish for Christians to just accept every illness (especially chronic illness) that comes along as the will of God for their lives without even asking Him if there is a spiritual cause for it. God will show them if there is; He wants them to overcome it. The scriptures clearly teach that while sickness may be permitted by God in the Christian's life at times, He has a definite purpose for allowing it. Once that purpose has been accomplished, however, one may expect the sickness to be healed.

Chapter Ten

Unbelief

A nother major hindrance to healing is unbelief. Unbelief is the result of wrong teaching or simply ignorance of the word of God. How can people believe in that of which they have not heard? God says, in Hosea 4:6, *"My people are destroyed for lack of knowledge..."* If people are not taught that healing is in the atonement, that it is available to them as God's children, and if they are not encouraged to expect it, they will have a hard time receiving their healing from God.

Does one have to have strong personal faith in order to be healed? Not always. Some people who lack faith of their own may be healed as someone else prays the prayer of faith for them. However, they may not be able to retain their healing without faith of their own, and because they are unable to retain their healing, they may soon doubt that they were ever healed.

In Jesus' day, some people came to Him seeking healing for themselves and some came desiring healing for someone dear to them. Jesus let it be known, in most instances, that it was faith that had effected the healing. Listen to what He had to say about the part faith played in those healings.

To the centurion who came on behalf of his sick servant, Jesus said, *"Go your way, and as you have believed, so let it be done for you"* (Matt. 8:13).

To the woman with the issue of blood—*"Be of good cheer, daughter; your faith has made you well"* (Matt. 9:22).

To the two blind men, *"According to your faith, let it be to you"* (Matt. 9:29).

To the Canaanite woman, who wanted healing for her daughter . . . *"O woman, great is your faith! Let it be as you desire* (Matt. 15:28).

In the case of the paralytic who was brought to Jesus by his four believing friends, The Bible says that he was saved and healed by their *faith* (Mark 2:5).

In James 5:15, it is written, that the *"prayer of faith will save the sick."* Jesus healed some who perhaps did not have *great* faith for healing, but they had enough faith to come to Him and make their petition known, hoping that He would grant their request. Yet some Christians do not have enough faith even to ask God for healing and it may be that they do not have healing because they do not ask for it (James 4:2)!

It is important to realize that when Jesus was here on earth, He healed everyone who *came to Him* for healing and even a few who did not. Now, people cannot go to Jesus in a physical sense but they can come to Him for salvation. Once they have done that, they can expect to receive all the benefits of that salvation (Ps. 103:2-3) as they follow Him in obedience and as their faith grows.

The Bible says that Christians are to *"work out"* their own salvation (Phil. 2:12). Of course, that does not mean that one works *for* his salvation. Eph. 2:8-9, and other scriptures show that salvation is a gift from God. It does mean that there are some things having to do with one's spiritual growth that one has to work at. If one wants to be a person of *"great faith"* (Matt. 15:28) instead of one of *"little faith"* (Matt. 6:30) or *"no faith"* (Mark 4:40), he will have to make a conscious effort to build up his faith and to exercise it so that it will grow.

There is a difference between having faith and *trying* to have faith. Many people act as if they have faith and say that they have faith (because they know they are supposed to have it) and they really want to have it. Yet, they do not have it because they do not know how to get it. Genuine faith comes from knowledge of the word of God. Romans 10:17 says *"...faith cometh by hearing and hearing by the word of God."* If one does not know what God says He will do in a certain situation, he cannot know what to believe Him for. Moreover, if one does not *believe* that He will do what He says He will do, there is no advantage in knowing what He has said.

One can understand people being ignorant of the word of God, but what is hard to understand is people that know what the word of God says and do not believe it! Hebrews 4:2 says that the word of God does not profit some people because the word "is not mixed with faith". As already noted, the kind of faith that is needed to receive *all* that God has for one is believing that God will do just what He has said in His word that He will do in *any given situation.*

The Bible talks about two different kinds of faith. There is a *gift* of faith (I Cor. 12:9) that is a special manifestation of The Holy Spirit's presence that is given, in certain situations where the will of God cannot be determined by the word of

God. But it is not a gift that one possesses permanently. It is a gift given to one by the Holy Spirit in a particular situation, at a particular time for a particular purpose. It is temporary—like the faith Elijah had when he stood against the 450 prophets of Baal, but did not have when he was threatened by Jezebel and so feared for his life (I Kings 18:1-19:3).

Then there is the *measure* of faith that is given to everyone at salvation. In fact, one cannot be saved without this measure of faith. Eph. 2:8 says that one is saved by grace through *faith*. This measure of faith grows by hearing the word of God (I Peter 1:23). God intends that one feeds this measure of faith with the word of God and exercises it by visible demonstrations until it becomes strong, lasting and unshakeable.

The word of God is medicine for unbelief. One should keep digesting it until doubt and unbelief are gone and faith has come and then he should keep digesting it to receive and maintain all that God has promised him. (Every Bible ought to have printed instructions on the outside cover—*"Take three times a day or as often as needed"*).

Once the sword of God's word cuts through all the doubt and unbelief in one's mind and gets down into his spirit, one will know he is healed, no matter what the doctor says, or his symptoms say, or what other people say.

While Jesus healed all who came to him for healing, He also healed some who did not come to Him and whose personal faith was not involved because someone else with great faith came to Jesus on their behalf, such as the Gentile woman's daughter (Mark 7: 25-30), the Nobleman's son (John 4:43-56), and the Centurion's servant (Matt. 8:1-13).

Then there were others who Jesus healed who not only did not come to Him but evidently did not have anyone else to go to Jesus on their behalf. He went to them instead— for instance, the man at Bethesda (John 5:1-15), the man in the synagogue with the withered hand (Luke 6: 6-10), the Gadarene demoniac (Luke 8:26-36).

Jesus healed the the leper whose faith was weak (Mark 1:40-42) and the epileptic boy whose father brought him to Jesus to be healed, but who confessed to Jesus that his faith was weak and asked Him to strengthen it.

Even today, God sometimes heals those who are out-side the kingdom of God, such as the Caananite woman's daughter (Matt. 15:21-28), or those whose faith is weak or non-existent. He does this when and where He chooses and for His own sovereign purposes. Sometimes it is to call atten-tion to the gospel and sometimes it is to confirm the gospel. Somtimes it is just to demonstrat His sovereignty, compas-sion or mercy. Those who are healed without their personal faith being involved or who are outside the kingdom of God are recipients of what some might call "*random*" healings.

Of course, the non-believer or the doubting Christian can never know if he will be granted one of these "*random*" healings or not. He can only hope that he might be, whereas the Bible makes it clear that *God promises healing to all who truly believe God's word and who will meet God's conditions. It is God's covenant with His people.* All of God's promises are yea and amen—never "*no*" or "*maybe*" (II Cor. 1:20).

The man at the pool of Bethesda that Jesus healed was only one of a multitude of sick people that were there that day. Yet the Bible only tells of the one man that Jesus healed. He was not a believer in Jesus because the Bible says that he did not know who it was that healed him. In fact, Jesus implied that he was a sinner by warning him after he had healed him to "*go and sin no more lest a worse thing come upon you*" (John 5:14).

This account has often been used by doubters who say that Jesus never healed every sick person with whom He came in contact. Nonetheless, the Bible is clear that Jesus healed all who *came to Him* for healing. Possibly, the one man that Jesus healed at Bethesda might have been the means of many others coming to Jesus for healing. In fact, this crowd of fellow sufferers no doubt was used to seeing this lame man lying at the pool time after time, perhaps for years. Because the Bible says he had had this condition for thirty-eight years, it is highly unlikely that those who knew this man would not have witnessed or heard of his healing and, as a result, sought Jesus out for their own healing. Perhaps Jesus performed this healing to get the attention of those at the pool so that He could preach to them about salvation and perhaps heal them.

The Bible gives many accounts of how one healing witnessed by many served to bring them to Jesus for salvation or healing. However, Jesus did not always need a crowd to spread His word, nor does He now. When Jesus went to Samaria, He did not go first into the city and preach to the crowds. He met one lone woman out of town at a well. Then, after He revealed Himself to her, *she* went into the town and spread the word of her encounter with Jesus to the occupants there, which resulted in many of those people coming to Jesus and receiving salvation.

Here is what the Bible says about the woman's testimony:

"And many of the Samaritans of that city believed in Him because of the word of the woman who testified—'He told me all that I ever did.' So when the Samaritans had come

*to Him, they urged Him to stay with them;
and he stayed there two days. **And many
more believed because of His own word"***
(John 4:39-41).

Sometimes it only takes one person being touched by God
to spread the word and inspire others to seek God's touch on
their lives. Jesus knows whom He can trust to do this.

Many of today's Christians have expressed that they are
unable to believe God for their healing because someone
they know and admire as a fellow believer, has had prayer
for healing and has not received it. That person may even
have died in their illness, in spite of much prayer. While that
is understandably puzzling, such occurrences do not render
God's word null and void. God's word is not interpreted by
one's own, or anyone else's, experiences.

Although one might not know why specific persons
did not receive the healing they desired, he can know from
God's word many general reasons why people do not receive
healing. The conclusion that it is not God's will to heal
everyone, *solely* because not all are healed, is one that is
widely held in much of the body of Christ. It must grieve the
heart of God greatly because that conclusion denies so much
of what He has said in His word thus hindering so many

from receiving God's promise of healing.

Would one conclude that it is not God's will to save everyone just because some people are not saved? Of course not—that is contrary to God's word. Neither should one conclude that God does not want everyone healed just because one knows some Christians who, *as yet*, have not been healed. Indeed, many things happen in the world today and even in the Church sometimes, that are contrary to God's word. Christian doctrine or theology is not formed by observing other people's circumstances or experiences, but solely by what the word of God has to say (II Tim. 3:16).

One must realize that he cannot really know the condition of another's heart, soul and mind no matter how much he might think he does. In recent years, there have been reports of the fall from grace of many well-known and beloved people of God because of a secret sin in their life that no one suspected was there.

Neither can anyone know the depths of another person's faith. Many people say they have faith because they know they are supposed to, when in reality they have deep-rooted doubts that cannot be ministered to, either because they do not realize that they have them or they will not acknowledge them.

Some people have remarked that they can believe God to meet their need in one area but not in others. This should not be. How can Christians believe *anything* God says if they cannot believe *all* that He says?

Some Christians say they can believe God for the healing of others but not for themselves. This is a contradiction—how can one truly pray the prayer of faith for another's healing if he believes that God makes *any* exceptions? The most likely explanation for this mindset is that it is rooted in feelings of unworthiness. As long as he is not deliberately sinning against God, he should expect God's promises to be fulfilled in his life as well as in anyone else's.

However, there are many situations where sickness is present that call for *corporate* prayer and faith, and perhaps even fasting, and it could very well be that the Body of Christ has failed its sick brothers and sisters by not under girding them this way (Exodus 17:10-13, Lev. 26:8, Matt. 17:21, Acts 12:5).

Later chapters will discuss other reasons why some people do not receive healing—but does one really need to know the answer to someone else's problem or situation in order to believe God for one's own? Surely not!

When Jesus was telling Peter what His will was for Peter's life, (John 21:15-22), Peter actually turned from Jesus and began to question what God's will was for John's life. Jesus sharply rebuked Peter for his failure to focus on what Jesus had said to Peter himself. There is a strong inference here that one can lose sight of what God has for that individual if one focuses on what is happening in other people's lives instead of focusing on what God has to say to him alone. What God is doing in someone else's life is not anyone's business but that individual's—that is between him and God—which is exactly what Jesus told Peter (verse 23).

Dr. Lillian Yeomans, in her book, *"His Healing Power,"* gives us an excellent scriptural answer to the question, "Why are some people not healed?" She writes:

> "There is an answer to every legitimate question in the Bible, and I find it in this case in Duet. 29:29—'The secret things belong unto the Lord our God; but those things which are revealed belong unto us and to our children forever, that we may do all the words of this law.' It is clearly revealed that Christ has redeemed us from the curse of the law (Gal. 3:13) including sickness to which man is liable. This truth belongs to us and our children and we are responsible before God of the use we make of it. Things that God has not seen fit to reveal to us at this time are not our property and we do well to remember

this and refrain from touching them even in thought." (p. 239-240)

In Matthew 14:25-31, Peter stepped out of the boat into the raging sea and began to walk on the water simply because he heard Jesus calling him to "Come." He did not stop to consider that he had never been able to walk on water before that time or that Jesus evidently had not said that to the other disciples because they were not making any move to get out of the boat. He just knew what Jesus had said to *him*, he responded to that word in faith and obedience, and found himself walking on the water just as Jesus did.

However, when he took his eyes off Jesus and began to observe what was going on around him—that the winds were "*boisterous*"—he began to sink. Jesus said that Peter had "*little faith.*"

Some Christians believe that God keeps them serving Him and dependent on Him by keeping them sick. These people probably sincerely believe what they are saying. Nevertheless, that is just the opposite of what God's word teaches—that God promises healing to those who serve and obey Him. Surely it's the love of God—His for the individual and the individual's love for Him—that should be the determining factor in whether or not one serves Him.

Chapter Eleven

Ignorance of Spiritual Warfare

There are those Christians who are doing all they know to please God, yet are suffering physical affliction unnecessarily simply because they do not understand spiritual warfare. Many Christians, surprisingly, are not taught that as soon as they become a born-again child of God, they also become engaged in a spiritual battle. Their enemy is Satan, the one Jesus said came, *"...to steal, and to kill, and to destroy"* (John 10:10).

At some time, Satan has attacked these Christians with sickness, and because they had no understanding of spiritual warfare, or of the will of God concerning healing, they just accepted that sickness as the will of God for their life. They do not realize that they can have victory over sickness by the power of Jesus' blood, His word, and His name.

Satan is constantly seeking to either hinder the believer from receiving God's blessings or to rob him of them once he has received them. His ultimate goal is to turn him away from God and keep the kingdom of God from growing through his testimony. If one is not aware that he has an enemy, much less aware of his tactics and the weapons he has been given to defeat him, he will fall victim to that enemy's deception and thievery.

Just to accept everything that happens as being the will of God for one's life, is to deny that he is engaged in a spiritual battle. Christians must realize that if they are being an effective witness for Christ, they will experience an attack of Satan occasionally. The Bible makes this very clear.

The apostle Paul says in Ephesians 6:10-18 that one can expect opposition from Satanic powers from time to time and warns believers to be prepared:

> *"Finally, my brethren, be strong in the Lord and in the power of His might. **Put on the whole armor of God, that you may be able to stand against the [tricks] of the devil.** For we do not wrestle against flesh and blood, but against principalities, against powers, against the rulers of the darkness of this age, against spiritual hosts of wickedness in the heavenly places. **Therefore take up the***

**whole armor of God, that you may be able to
stand in the evil day.** *Stand therefore, having
girded your waist with truth, having put on
the breastplate of righteousness, and having
your feet shod with the gospel of peace;* **above
all, taking the shield of faith, with which you
will be able to quench all the fiery darts of
the wicked one.** *And take the helmet of salvation, and* **the sword of the Spirit, which is the
word of God."**

He also admonishes Timothy, in I Tim. 6:12, to *"[f]ight
the good fight..."* Paul says of himself, in II Tim. 4:7,

*"I have fought the good fight, I have finished
the race, I have kept the faith."*

The apostle Peter writes:

*"Be sober, be vigilant; because your
adversary the devil walks about like a
roaring lion, seeking whom he may devour.*
Resist him, steadfast in the faith ..."
(1 Peter 5:8-9a).

God does not call anyone to be a passive Christian, but to *"...contend earnestly for the faith..."* (Jude 3). In any army, those who refuse to fight will eventually become deserters, prisoners or casualties. Rather, God has called believers to be overcomers (I John 5:4) and to be *"...more than conquerors..."* (Romans 8:37). One need not fear the attacks of the enemy for God has promised the victory to the one *who is submitted to God and resists the enemy* (James 4:7). Furthermore, Jesus said that He has given his followers power over all the power of the enemy (Luke 10:19).

One of the most common ways that Satan attacks the children of God is with sickness. Instead of recognizing and resisting Satan attacks, believers often surrender to them, thinking that they are surrendering to the will of God for their lives.

In addition, even after one has received healing, Satan will try to rob him of it by attacking him with the same old symptoms. If Satan can get one to doubt his healing, he can afflict him again.

Of course, not every discomfort that one experiences can be blamed on the work of Satan. When sickness (especially chronic sickness) comes into the believer's life, he needs to inquire of God as to whether he has brought it on himself, whether God is allowing it for a purpose (perhaps to get one's attention about something?), or if he is being attacked by Satan in an attempt to disrupt or discredit the believer's ministry.

God will give the answer if one is sincerely willing to hear what He has to say. God has promised abundant wisdom for the asking (James 1:5). He has also given the discernment of the Holy Spirit (I Cor. 12:10), so that one might be able to distinguish between the working of his own flesh, God's working in his life or Satan's working.

Satan often foolishly exposes himself as the source of one's physical discomfort by the use of his well-known and well-worn tactics. They are as old as the Garden of Eden. He will try to convince Christians that God did not say what He said, did not mean what He said or that what God said does not apply to them. He will try to portray God as less than a good God, as he did to Eve. He even will try to distract Christians from the will of God by offering them the *"rewards"* of sin as he offered Eve in the garden and Jesus in the wilderness (Gen. 3:5, Luke 4:5-7).

In taking a stand of resistance against Satan's attack, one must develop some tactics and strategies of his own. First, one must be sure that he has submitted himself to God (James 4:7). Then, he must use the word of God as a sword against his enemy, as Jesus did in the wilderness (Matt. 4:1-11) and as he is instructed to in Eph. 6:17. If a Christian does not know what the word of God says concerning Satan's attack, whether it is sickness, fear, finances, etc., he will not be able to withstand the enemy.

The truth is, Satan knows what the word of God says but he also knows that if he can keep one ignorant of the word, confuse one with it, or cause one to doubt it, he can prevent its working in the Christian's life. One must let Satan know that not only does he know what the Word says, but that he understands its true intent, as Jesus also did.

Here are some simple spiritual exercises that are very effective in counteracting the deceptive plan of the enemy. Although the following exercises principally refer to healing, they can be adapted to whatever type of spiritual battle Christians may find themselves in.

1. One should memorize or write down as many of God's healing promises as one can find in God's word. Many of them are quoted in this book but more can be discovered with the use of a good Biblical concordance. It is also good to memorize or write down those scriptures that teach Christians that they have power over Satan's power.

2. Then, instead of pleading with God to give them

something He has already promised them, and using their list, they should begin to thank and praise Him for the fulfillment of each of those promises, no matter how one feels.

The following is a *sample* of a type of thanksgiving/warfare prayer, although one should word his prayer according to his own convictions. It does not need to be particularly lengthy—it is one's faith in what he is declaring that will enable him to overcome sickness, not the amount of words he says):

My Father God, I thank you that You always were, always are and always will be the God Who Heals Me. I thank You, Jesus, that it is Your will and the will of Your Father to heal all that will believe You for it. I thank you, that You forgive all my sin and heal all of my diseases. I thank You, God, that Your word says that many are the afflictions of the righteous but the Lord delivers me out of them all.

I thank you, Father, that it is Your good

pleasure to give me the kingdom. There is no sickness in your kingdom because Jesus sent His disciples to preach the gospel, heal the sick and tell people that the kingdom of God had come unto them. Father, You said that You would not withhold any good thing from them that walk uprightly. As far as I can judge myself I am walking uprightly and I believe healing is one of the good things You said You would not withhold from me.

I thank You, Jesus, that You bore my sickness so I would not have to. I thank and praise You, Jesus, I am no longer under the curse of sickness because You took my curse upon Yourself. I thank You, Jesus, that by Your stripes I am healed.

I thank You, Jesus, that You came to this earth with healing in Your wings for all those that fear Your name. I do fear your name, Lord. I thank You, Jesus, that there is healing power in Your name. Your name is as ointment poured forth. I thank and praise You that there is healing power in Your word. I say with the Psalmist, that "unless Your law had been my delight I would have perished in my affliction" but because I love Your word, it will be health to my flesh and strength to my bones.

I thank You, Father, that You have said that no weapon formed against me shall prosper. I thank you, Jesus, that you have given me power over all the power of the enemy. I believe this sickness (name it) is an attack of Satan and I take authority over him and over this sickness (name it) by the power of God's word and that Name that is above every other name—Jesus. I command Satan and this sickness (name it) to flee from me and for my body to line up with the word of God.

I thank you for my healing, Lord, and I receive it in Jesus' name even though I don't see it or feel it as yet. I know it's coming and I promise, Lord, to use my health and strength for Your purpose in my life. I will be a witness to Your saving, healing power and give You all the glory!

This type of prayer should be prayed aloud so Satan can hear it, too, and he will know that the one praying knows the Word and is standing on it. The believer himself needs to hear it, as well, so his faith can grow because,

> "...*faith cometh by hearing and hearing by the word of God*" (Romans 10:17).

In addition, there is a power that is released in audible prayer that is not present in silent prayer. The Bible tells us in Ps. 22:3 that God inhabits (resides in) the praises of His people. Because God dwells in the believer, when he praises out loud, he releases God's power and presence from within himself into the atmosphere around him where Satan resides, causing the enemy to flee (Eph. 2:2). When Satan hears one praising God for all that He is and all He has done and can do, Satan is reminded of his own limited power and also his ultimate fate. It torments him and he will not remain in that atmosphere.

It also pleases God greatly to hear his children declare their faith in His word, and when He is pleased with them, He will move mightily on their behalf. If one is walking in obedience to God, striving to please Him in all that he does or says, he has every right to claim God's healing promises and expect the fulfillment of those promises to manifest in his life.

Chapter Twelve

Unwillingness to Let Go

As strange as it may seem, some people, either consciously or subconsciously, do not really want to get well. They may even ask for prayer for healing at times and yet not be ready to receive that healing for one reason or another. They may enjoy or need the attention and sympathy that their illness, or even receiving prayer, brings to them.

Some people use their illness to control others and they might not be ready to relinquish that control. Others may use their illness to avoid the responsibility that might become theirs if they were well. Some may even be reluctant to part with some financial benefit that their illness provides them.

As long as one uses his illness to serve his self-interest, he is demonstrating that he is not yet ready to part with it and he gives his sickness permission to linger in his life. One cannot claim healing in one breath and sickness in another — whichever serves one best at the moment.

Jesus asked the man with the infirmity at the pool of Bethesda, *"Do you want to be whole?"* Why would Jesus, who knew men's heart's and minds, ask this question when He already knew the answer? He asked the question because He wanted the man to think about what it would mean to him to be whole and if he was ready to assume that responsibility.

If one truly wants to be healed, he must be sure that he is not finding his sickness useful to him in any of the ways mentioned above. He may be doing that without realizing it, so he must ask the Holy Spirit to show him his own heart in this matter. He may have to work a little at *not* using his sickness for his own purpose before healing comes. Additionally, one must guard one's confession. The Bible says that words have power to bring life or death even to one's self (Pro. 18:21). Satan and His evil spirits feed on one's words of self-pity, discouragement, doubt, fear, hopelessness, and self-centeredness, etc. As a result, the enemy is empowered by those negative words and attitudes to continue his hold on the sick one.

Proverbs 6:2 and Proverbs 12:13 says that anyone can become snared (trapped) by the words of their mouth. If an individual talks about his sickness constantly, he affirms the the presence and power of that sickness in his life. If he would receive healing from God, he must resist the temptation to do this. Instead, he should begin to declare God's healing promises over his life and demonstrate his faith in whatever ways God might require of him.

Chapter Thirteen

Our Way or God's Way

Some people do not receive their healing simply because they want to choose the method by which their healing comes. Naaman was the commander of the Syrian army (II Kings 5:1-15). The Bible tells us that he was a great and honorable man in the eyes of the king— *"a mighty man of valor."* Unfortunately, he was also a leper. His young Jewish servant girl told Naaman about the prophet Elisha in Samaria who could heal his disease.

When Naaman went to see Elisha, the prophet did not even come out of his house to meet him. Elisha sent a mere servant to tell Naaman to go and wash in the very muddy river Jordan seven times and then he would be healed. (Elisha evidently did not know what a great and honorable man Naaman was—or maybe he did!)

At first, Naaman resisted the instructions he was given. He had supposed that Elisha would come out to him and call out to God, wave his hand over Naaman's body and he would be healed. The Bible says that Naaman actually became furious that Elisa did not do that and that he went away in a rage. Evidently, he felt it beneath his station in life to do what Elisha told him to do. After all, there were cleaner rivers nearby that Naaman could have bathed in.

But Naaman's servant began to plead with him and finally convinced him to swallow his pride and do as he was told. Nathan's humility and obedience not only brought him healing, but the healing resulted in his becoming a true believer in the God of Israel as well (II Kings 5:15).

Although Jesus could have healed everyone by just pro-nouncing them healed, He chose to use a variety of methods in His healing ministry. There were those to whom simply spoke a healing word (Luke 5:24, Mark 5:41, 7:29, Mark 18:42). Some were healed by His touch alone (Matt. 8:1-3, 8:14-15, 9:29, 20:30, Luke 6:10). Others were healed as they touched the hem of His garment (Mark 5:25-34, Mark 6:56). Jesus used both his touch and His spoken word in the healing of the woman who had a spirit of infirmity that caused her to have a permanently bowed back (Luke 13:12-13).

In the case of the man who was deaf and had a speech impediment (Mark 7:32-35), Jesus put His finger in the man's ears, then He spat and touched the man's tongue before He spoke His healing word to him. Jesus led the blind man, in Mark 8:22-25, out of town. Then, the Bible tells us, He spit on the man's eyes, put his hand on him, after which the man regained partial sight. Then Jesus put His hand on his eyes again and made him look up. When he did, he saw everyone clearly.

Before Jesus healed the blind man in John 9:1-11, He spat on the ground and made clay with His saliva. Then, He anointed the eyes of the blind man with the clay and told him to go wash in the pool of Siloam. The Bible says that when the blind man did what Jesus told him to do, he "came back seeing."

Jesus made it very clear that some sicknesses are the result of demonic activity or influence in one's life. In Mark, 9:17-29, Jesus recognized that a demonic spirit troubled this boy who had seizures, therefore, instead of speaking the words, *"be thou made whole,"* or just touching the boy, Jesus commanded the spirit to come out of him. Previously the disciples had tried, but failed, to cast the evil spirit out. Jesus let it be known that some spirits, or perhaps their hold on an individual, are so strong that they can only be cast out by much prayer and fasting beforehand. Jesus discerned that what was needed in this situation was deliverance as well as healing. (Christians must have that same Holy Spirit discernment operating in their lives if they are to be effective in the healing ministry. They must also recognize, and utilize, the power of prayer *and* fasting.)

Matt. 9:32-33, Luke 13:11-13, Matt. 8:16, Mark 1:32-34, are all scriptures indicating that some situations where there are physical problems call for the casting out of evil spirits as well a prayer for healing. Acts 10:38 tells us that Jesus went about doing good and *"healing all who were oppressed of the devil."*

Why did Jesus use these various methods of healing with people when His words alone would have been enough? Was Jesus demonstrating to his followers that they should not expect all healings to come in the same way? Was He using the method of healing in a particular person's case based on that person's spiritual need? Did He have other purposes that He wanted to accomplish through the healing than just meeting the physical need of the one healed? *The answer to these last three questions is "Yes."*

One may be expecting and looking for an immediate or miraculous healing, while God's plan is that he should receive his healing gradually as he grows in faith and obedience—the lepers in Luke 17:14 were healed *as they went.*

Some years ago, before I became a Christian, I was troubled with severe migraine headaches. They happened to me on a regular basis—I would have one about every two weeks and they would last for about thirty-six hours during which I could not sleep, or even lie down, because of the pain. About a year after I became a Christian, I suddenly realized that I had not had a migraine for several months. This was over 45 years ago and I have never had another migraine. I could not tell exactly when my healing came, but I am convinced that God healed me gradually by means of a totally changed life-style which was the result my decision to follow Christ.

The way God chooses to bring healing to people *often depends on what additional purposes God may want to accomplish through their healing.* There may be times when God would have one take advantage of the excellent medical knowledge and skill that He has given to mankind. There may be other times when God would have one trust Him alone for his healing.

A word of caution: It is foolish to claim a faith one really does not have, and it can be very hazardous to one's health! Also, one certainly should never encourage anyone else to claim a faith that they do not have. Some people are able to trust God alone for healing so that they rarely, if ever, have to seek medical attention. But if one is not absolutely certain that God is asking him to depend on God alone for his healing, he should not hesitate to seek medical help when he needs it. There is nothing wrong with doing that as long as one does not leave God out of the situation and acknowledges His word as the final authority in his life.

Even if one's faith in God's direct healing touch is strong, God may still have an individual seek medical help, at times. Then, when his healing comes, it can be verified, if necessary, by an earthly authority that unbelievers and scoffers will respect and believe.

Much of the time, God requires cooperation in granting an individual's healing. That could mean disciplining one's self by taking better care of his body, letting go of his ungodly emotions or repenting of his neglect of spiritual exercise or other known sins. One's healing may not come until he does, or becomes willing to do, whatever the Lord asks of him— just as with the blind man whom Jesus told to go wash in the pool of Siloam (John 9:1-11). Jesus may require one to forgive someone, or to right the wrongs one has done, not only by asking forgiveness but by making restitution wherever, and if, possible.

One may have to let Jesus lead him *"out of town"*, like He did the blind man in Mark 8:22-25. One may be in a place spiritually or physically where God does not want him to be and needs to get out of there before his healing comes. If one is in a church that does not teach healing or offer prayer for healing, he may need to be willing to change churches or at least attend a few services somewhere where prayer for healing is offered and healings are happening.

People who attend churches that teach about healing and that encourage their people to expect healing, will have greater faith for healing than people who attend churches where healing is not taught, expected or practiced. In many churches, where the people worship God wholeheartedly and unashamedly and the Holy Spirit is allowed to move in the services as He wills, many people have been healed without anyone laying their hands on them or praying for them. That is because *"...the power of the Lord was present to heal them"* (Luke 5:17).

Sometimes, healing may depend just on one's change of attitude. He may find it too humbling to ask others to pray for him or to submit himself to be anointed with oil. Yet that could be the very thing that will bring about his healing. God may sometimes require him to share his need for healing with others that they might also share in his victory.

The book of Ecclesiastes tells us that there is a *time* to heal. God's timing is not always man's timing. Just because a person has been seeking God for healing for some time and has not *yet* been healed does not mean that he will not be.

John 11:1-45, tells the story of Jesus' raising Lazarus from the dead. Lazarus' sisters, Mary and Martha, sent word to Jesus that their brother Lazarus was sick. Now the Bible says in verse five, that Jesus loved Mary, Martha and Lazarus. One would think, that being the case, that Jesus would have come to the rescue right away. However, verse six tells us that Jesus stayed where He was for two more days. It must have taken Him an additional two days to travel to Bethany, the home of Lazarus and his sisters, because when He finally got there, Lazarus was dead and had been lying in the tomb for four days.

Martha was a little upset with Jesus. She said, *"Lord, if you had been here my brother would not have died"* (verse 21). Martha knew that Jesus had the power to heal, but she was about to get a revelation of another dimension of Jesus' eternal nature.

He said to her, *"...Your brother will rise again"* (verse 23). She replied that she knew her brother would rise in the last day. Then Jesus spoke to her this amazing word, *"...I [AM] the Resurrection and the Life..."* (verse 25). Martha and Mary both, as well as the others surrounding them, were about to discover that whatever Jesus would be, He already was. He is the eternal I AM! He is neither defined by, nor limited by, time.

Some of the crowd said, in verse 27, *"Could not this Man, who opened the eyes of the blind, also have kept this*

151

man from dying?" Yes, He could have, but Jesus wanted the people to understand that He was even greater than what they thought He was or what they expected Him to do. Eph. 3:20 says,

> *"...God is able to do exceedingly, abundantly above all that we can ask or think..."*

God wants present day Christians to understand, too, that He can bring life from things long dead. He can bring hope when all looks lost. Death has no power over the Lord, whether it is threatening the physical body, or seemingly ruling in a relationship or any other situation. Had Jesus come to Bethany as quickly as it was hoped and expected that He would, His healing of Lazarus would have confirmed what the people there already knew, that He is the Healer, but they may never have known that He is also, *now,* the Resurrection and the Life, as well as the Healer.

In John 9:45, the apostle says that many people came to believe in Jesus because of His raising Lazarus from the dead. God's delay in healing usually has a higher purpose than one's physical comfort. God may have an instantaneous healing for someone or He may have a path to healing for one to follow.

An occasion of sickness should always cause one to draw closer to his Healer asking for understanding as to what God is doing in his life and asking for direction as to what, if anything, one can do to cooperate with God's working in one's life. In fact, that is the most important thing one can do. In the Bible, those who were healed by touching the hem of Jesus' garment or by His touch had to make a determined effort to draw close to Him.

Some Christians believe it is wrong to question God and that they are being more spiritual if they do not do that. But the Bible encourages Christians to seek wisdom and understanding, especially in the book of Proverbs. Of course, God may not tell His children everything they would like to know, but if a situation needs one's cooperation, He will not keep him in the dark. Regardless of how healing comes or when, one can expect it eventually as he stays submitted to God because God has promised it to His children. Until it comes, one can rest in those promises.

Chapter Fourteen

Inherited Sicknesses

Some people feel that they are destined to be plagued with a certain chronic disease or physical weakness throughout their lifetime because that certain condition *"runs in the family."* That may be true outside of God's kingdom but it need not be true for the Christian.

When one comes to Christ and yields his life to Him, he becomes a new creation. Old things pass away and all things become new (II Cor. 5:17). He is born again as a child of God and made a joint-heir with Jesus Christ. His life is then guided and shaped by spiritual truths, and not by worldly philosophy, dictates, theories or concepts.

The truth that now applies to a new Christian's life is that God has promised healing to all of His children through the atonement of Christ's death on the cross. It does not matter how many in one's family has been afflicted with a certain disease or how long it has been in the family. All one needs to do is meet God's conditions for healing and then claim his rightful inheritance.

No Christian needs to live in fear of developing diabetes, heart problems, cancer, Alzheimer's, mental illness, etc., just because one of his parents had it. But if he does not know that, he might just fear it enough to bring it on. Job said that the thing he greatly feared had come upon him (Job 3:25). (Whether he knew it or not, when President Franklin Roosevelt told American citizens that they had nothing to fear but fear itself; he was giving people a spiritual principal by which to live their lives).

Some people who have had a parent die at a certain age believed that they, too, were destined to die at that same age—and they did so, because they believed it so strongly. That kind of thinking is purely superstition and has no place in a Christian's life or thought. Yet the Bible says that a Christian's thoughts are powerful. Pro. 23:7 says that whatever a man thinks he is in his heart, he is.

When I was a fairly new Christian and not yet very knowledgeable in God's word, I had a fear of going insane. Mainly because my grandmother had died in an insane asylum and I heard someone say that insanity, or mental illness, sometimes skips a generation. Although I had siblings, I thought I would be the logical one to receive the "inheritance" because at the time I did have a lot of confusion in my mind and did not understand what was causing it. I thought, *"I must be going out of my mind."* I even thought God had revealed this fate to me and I became very afraid of what was to come.

Before I came to Christ, I was searching desperately for some answers to life's problems and questions. I studied different world philosophies, religions, astrology, reincarnation and other various belief systems. I got very confused about what to believe and what to pursue, and what I did pursue did not seem to work for me. I even decided to make up my own philosophy to live by which was a mixture of my childhood Christian beliefs and a little bit of everything else I had studied. That did not work for me either. No wonder I was confused and seemed to be struggling to maintain my sanity!

One day, after I became a Christian, I came across a scripture in II Tim. 1:7, which reads:

*"For God has not given us the spirit of fear, but of power and of love and of a **sound mind**."*

I knew then that it was not God who had been speaking to me about going insane. Once I realized that, I claimed the sound mind that was my rightful inheritance as a child of God. The fear quickly left me and the confusion eventually left, too, as God gave me understanding of what was happening in my life. I soon learned that only the Word of God has the truth about life—one's origin, purpose, destiny and all that one needs to know about everyday living. It took awhile for the Word of God to cleanse my mind of all that confusion and for me to learn to discern truth from error.

The Bible says that Christians are *"...transformed by the renewing of their mind..."*

(Romans 12:2) and that they *"...shall know the truth and the truth shall make* [them] *free* (John 8:32). Until one learns what God has to say, he does not realize how much of his thinking is total deception or how much that deception has warped his view of life and how much it has limited his potential. *"Inherited sickness"* has no claim on the child of God who follows Him wholeheartedly and trusts in His promises.

Chapter Fifteen

Sickness — An Occasion for God's Glory?

There are members of the body of Christ who believe that they are suffering physical illness for the glory of God. They base their belief on the account of the healing of the blind man in John 9:1-3. A close examination of that passage should determine if that belief is true or not.

> *"Now as Jesus passed by, He saw a man who was blind from birth. And His disciples asked Him, saying, 'Rabbi, who sinned, this man or His parents, that he was born blind?' Jesus answered, 'Neither this man nor his parents sinned, but **that the works of God should be revealed in him."***

Of course, Jesus is not saying here that the man or his parents were sinless. They were not, because the Bible says that all have sinned and come short of God's glory (Romans 3:23). What Jesus was saying was that the man's blindness was not the direct result of any particular sin that he or his parents had committed. Then He reveals the reason for the man's blindness:

> *"... that the works of God might be revealed in him" (John 1:3).*

What are the works of God? The Bible says that the works of God are to *save, heal and deliver*. When the blind man was healed, he was a tremendous witness to God's power to perform those works. Had Jesus not healed the man of his blindness, the works of God would not have been demonstrated in him, and God would not have been glorified. Therefore, God is not glorified in sickness but in healing.

Notice that in the account of Jesus' healing of the paralytic, all the people who witnessed it *"were amazed and **glorified** God, saying, 'we never saw anything like this'"* (Mark 2:12).

Matthew 15:31 says this:

> *"So the multitudes marveled when they saw*
> *the mute speaking, the maimed made whole,*
> *the lame walking, and the blind seeing: and*
> *they **glorified** the God of Israel."*

After Jesus raised the widow's son from the dead, in Luke Chapter 7, the scriptures say:

> *"Then fear came upon all, and they **glorified***
> *God saying, 'A great prophet has risen up*
> *among us' and '**God** has visited His people'"*
> (verse 16).

In Luke chapter 13, when Jesus healed the woman who had had a spirit of infirmity for eighteen years, not only did she *glorifiy God after she was healed,* but verse 17 says that Jesus' adversaries were put to shame and all the multitude rejoiced for all the *glorious things* that were done by Him. In addition, Luke 17: 15 says that when the leper was healed, he *glorified God.*

Some Christians have stated that a Christian who bears their physical suffering sweetly and patiently can be a witness for Christ in their suffering. It is true that God can use an individual for some purpose wherever he is in his faith or his circumstances. God may be grieved that one is unable to receive all that God has for him, but He does not disown anyone because of it. He meets everyone where his faith is.

Nevertheless, how often do people hear of someone coming to Christ because they knew someone who was sick compared to the reports of those who come to believe on Christ because someone they knew was healed?

As many others have pointed out, if one really believes that sickness was God's will for his life, bearing his illness patiently would mean that he would not be so quick to run to the doctor to be treated or to get medicine to relieve it or get rid of it altogether.

When Christians are healed, they are a witness not only to the peace and to the patience God can give, but they are also a witness to God's will for mankind, His faithfulness to His word, His compassion, His divinity, His sovereignty, and His resurrection power! So which really witnesses to *all* that God is—sickness or healing?

Some people say that healing is not that important—that salvation is the "real" miracle. Naturally, healing of the body is not as important as the salvation of the soul. However, when someone is healed by God of an incurable disease, that is a miracle, too, which brings God glory and often leads to the salvation of souls. Christians should never minimize this work of God.

In Acts chapter 3:1 through Acts 4:4, when Peter and John ministered healing to the lame man at the gate of the temple, the lame man's joy and excitement was such that the people came running to witness this great miracle in the life of one they knew so well. Peter and John were then able to preach the gospel to this vast crowd with such conviction that about five thousand of them became believers.

In addition, when Peter raised Tabitha from the dead, *"… it became known throughout all Joppa and many believed on the Lord"* (Acts 9: 42). John 11:45 also says that many people came to believe in Jesus because of Lazarus' resurrection from the dead.

If one feels that he is sick for God's glory, then he should be expecting to be healed eventually. God is glorified when His power and sovereignty is seen and felt in the earth and demonstrated through the lives of His children.

Chapter Sixteen

"Faith Healers"

There are those, both within and without the Body of Christ, who have nothing but contempt for what they call "*faith healers*." This has become a popular, yet somewhat demeaning term (unfortunately) for those evangelists whose ministries include praying for the sick and encouraging people to believe God for physical healing as well as for salvation.

A thorough study of many well-known "*faith healers*" and some that are not so well known, shows that there have been a few of them who have used the healing aspect of the gospel to take advantage of others and to feather their own nests. This is a tragic reality. Others have used unwise or hard-to-understand methods in their ministering to others which has caused some people to be wary of "*faith healers*." Many even go so far as to refuse to have anything to do with the subject of Biblical healing.

Nevertheless, to brand all *"faith healers"* as fakes, charlatans, false prophets and false teachers and their ministries as demonic, as some people have done, is a dangerous thing. Not only were Peter, John, Paul, Philip and other disciples *"faith healers"* but Jesus Himself was one as well. He always encouraged people to have faith for healing, and He always responded to those who did have faith for healing by healing them. It was the religious people (Pharisees) of His day that accused Jesus of healing and doing other miracles by the power of Satan (Matt. 12:22-24). Comparatively, it is usually the religious people of today that are most critical of *"faith healers."*

Some people say that all who claim to be healed do not stay healed, so the healing they claimed to have received could not have been genuine. One critic, Sandy Simpson, (2009), in an on-line article entitled *Biblical Divine Healing Versus other Types of Healing*, states that when Jesus healed people they stayed healed. (Biblical Divine Healing section, para 1) But that is not true according to the scriptures. Jesus warned the man at the pool of Bethesda that if he did not refrain from sinning, a *"worse affliction would come upon [him]"* (John 5: 14). By this example, Jesus was letting His followers know of one circumstance in which people might not retain their healing. Also, if one does not know how to do spiritual warfare or deliberately sins against God, the enemy can steal the blessings of God from him. In John 10:10, the Bible states that the enemy comes ...*to steal, to kill, and to destroy."* I Peter 5:8 says that *"the devil walks about... seeking whom he may devour."*

Ms. Simpson further states that *"faith healers"* sometimes tell people to *"empty their minds"* or *"leave their minds at the door."* (Psychological section, para. 5) In the forty-six years that I have been Christian, I have attended many healing services in various places led by various people, and I have never heard anyone give similar instructions to someone who was seeking healing. One can only surmise that Ms. Simpson's experience with faith healers was very limited. It is unfortunate that Ms. Simpson's experience with *"faith healers"* was one where such an ungodly thing took place, because it evidently soured her on *"faith healers"* forever.

Some critics of faith healing even go so far as to doubt the genuineness of a healing ministry because of the joy and excitement that seeing people healed by God often generates! (Makes one wonder what it takes to make some people get happy and excited!). Some critics, no doubt, would have complained about the lame man who, after Peter and John healed him at the temple gate, went walking and leaping

and praising God (Acts 3:1-10). Those same critics, probably would have been among the religious people who, upon
hearing the crowd rejoicing and praising God with *"loud
voices"* as Jesus entered Jerusalem on His way to the cross,
tried to get Jesus to rebuke His disciples for what the critics
considered an excessive display of emotion. Jesus simply
replied:

> *"...if these should keep silent, the stones
> would **immediately** cry out"* (Luke 19:37-40).

Ms. Simpson also argues that in order for a healing to
be *"divine"* (evidently that means directly from God with no
help from doctors or medicine), it has to be a healing from an
incurable disease that, of course, would be a miracle healing.
(Biblical Divine Healing section, para. 2) Did Jesus only perform miraculous healings? The Bible says that Jesus healed
all kinds of sickness and *all kinds* of diseases (Matt. 4:23).
Not only that, He even gave his disciples instructions to heal
all kinds of sickness and *all kinds* of disease (Matt.10:11).

There were physicians in Jesus' day. Can it not be
assumed that there were some people then whose illnesses
could have been healed by physicians if they had had the
means to afford their services? Would they not have come

166

to Jesus, seeking healing and would Jesus have refused them because their disease was not an incurable one? The Bible says that Jesus healed all who came. Would Jesus refuse to heal those today whose diseases probably could be cured by doctors and medicine but who cannot afford the treatment?

When I was a child, people did not have good health insurance like they do now. Our family would probably have been considered poor by today's standards. We had no extra money for medical emergencies. I do not remember a doctor ever coming to our house (yes, doctors did that in those depression years). But I remember many times when different members of our family, being ill, were taken to church and anointed with oil and prayed for by the elders for all kind of things from which we always recovered.

Yes, *"faith healers"* sometimes make mistakes and do unwise things. And the body of Christ is very good at *"throwing out the baby with the bath water."* Some preachers will not preach about hell at all because they feel other Christians over-emphasize it. Others will not preach grace because, in their opinion, some preach it too much and make it sound *"cheap"*. Some preachers and teachers will have nothing to do with certain spiritual gifts because they feel others put too much emphasis on them. *Then there are those who do not teach or practice what the Bible says about healing because some do not do it perfectly.* (Perhaps they are afraid that they will not do it perfectly either, and will not have the results they should).

The fact that some Christians over-emphasize some Biblical truths, even to the total neglect of others, or mishandle them, is not a valid reason for other Christians to neglect to believe and practice those same truths. It is just as out-of-balance to be lacking these components of the Gospel altogether in one's life and church services as it is to over-emphasize them or misuse them. No one is going to be held accountable for how other people handle the things of God, only how they themselves do. (People who will have nothing to do with the healing ministry because some people do not handle it right are as much in error as those people who say they do not vote because they feel that all politicians are corrupt.)

If pastors do not teach about healing in their churches, or pray for the sick, they are not preaching the whole gospel and are failing their flock. They will one day be held accountable. Ezekiel 34:1-9 pronounces a woe (calamity) upon those shepherds who feed themselves and not the flock (verse 8). Verse four reads, in part, *"The weak you have not strengthened, nor have you healed those who were sick ..."*

Sick people are going to congregate wherever they think they will find hope and faith and power to meet their need.

168

Consequently, it makes one wonder—if more pastors and elders were willing to anoint the sick with oil (as the Bible says they should do) and were able to pray a genuine prayer of faith over them, would people still feel the need to flock to a "*faith healer*"? Would "*faith healers*" still be needed to travel the world and draw the great crowds that they do?

Who better than one's own pastor or local church leaders, who have been entrusted with that individual's spirtual growth and who should know their congregations well, to help them receive and retain all that God has for them? Until pastors practice the anointing with oil for healing in their churches, people will continue to seek out faith healers.

It may seem puzzling to some that many preachers and evangelists who pray for the sick, do not usually preach on healing, (at least not very often), but rather preach salvation after which they give an invitation for people to receive Christ. Then they either pray for the sick as Jesus told His followers to do, or people find that they are healed without anyone touching them. That is good and that is scriptural—*It is God confirming His word with signs followings!* (Mark 16:17-18).

However, many people come away from healing meetings disappointed and confused because they do not understand all that has taken place. There is possibly a way that

some of that can be avoided. There have been many evangelistic crusades where scores of people have responded to an
invitation to receive Christ. Those people are often given a
booklet with instructions on how to maintain their salvation
and grow in Christ. Why should not the same type of instruction be given to those who come forward in churches and
other Christian gatherings for prayer for healing?

People need to be taught what the Bible has to say
about healing, how to prepare one's self to receive healing
and why some people are not healed or do not retain their
healing. They also need to understand that even the people
Jesus healed were not all healed instantly. For one man, at
least, it took more than one touch from Jesus for his healing
to be completed (Mark 8:24) and some were healed as they
went (Luke 17:14), which is gradual healing. So just because
we do not see everyone who is prayed for healed *instanta-
neously*, it does not mean that they were not healed.

In addition, people need to be instructed that if their sickness is the result of a sinful life-style, then they need to forsake that sin in order to retain their healing—just as Jesus
admonished the man at the pool of Bethesda (John 5:14).
They also need to be taught spiritual warfare, how it relates
to healing and how and when to engage in that warfare. Most
of all, they need to know what the Bible says about healing

so that their faith for healing will be based on the word of God and not on someone else's faith or words.

Many people who pray for the sick have great faith and zeal but lack wisdom and discernment. They need instruction, too. There is a little more to the healing ministry than just laying hands on someone and declaring them healed, just as salvation involves more that just making a profession with one's mouth. *Zeal without knowledge can do great damage to the people one ministers to, as well as doing great damage to the cause of Christ and His Church.*

There was recently a situation where a lady was very seriously ill and her loved ones called for a minister to come and pray for her healing. After prayer, this minister told the lady and her loved ones that she was healed. However, the lady herself did not feel that she was healed—in fact, she died shortly afterward. Her loved ones were so upset that from that moment on they would have nothing to do with the ministry of healing or "*faith healers.*"

It probably is unwise to tell people that they are healed. If the person is healed, he will know it, either in his body or his spirit. Whenever possible, healings should be confirmed by one's physician, except perhaps in a situation where it is obvious to everyone acquainted with the healed person that healing has come.

However, the minister in the above situation was not necessarily a "*fake*" who was claiming a power he did not have or deliberately deceiving the lady and her family. His own faith in God's power and willingness to heal may have been so strong and vibrant that he thought surely God would heal her. Yet, the lady may not have had the faith to be healed. In Acts 14:8-10 there is an account of Paul ministering healing to a lame man at Lystra after he *perceived* that the man had "*...faith to be healed.*" Or, like some of the people Jesus ministered to (Mark 2: 1-5, 10-11), the lady's greatest need might have been for salvation and that need should have been ministered to first.

*Those whose compassion for the sick and whose calling and genuine desire is to minister the things of God to others, **must** seek, and rely upon, the direction of God as they minister.* This is where the gifts of the Holy Spirit, such as the gift of discernment, the word of knowledge, the word of wisdom, etc., operating in their ministries can be very beneficial in letting them know how to minister in certain situations. The Holy Spirit, through these gifts, can help to discern the spiritual level of the one being ministered to, their ability to receive the things of God, and just how one ought to pray.

If the spiritual state of the one needing healing cannot be discerned, it is usually best to talk to them about their relationship with God before offering a healing prayer. If the person is not a Christian, their illness might be the very thing that God is using to help them see their need for salvation. One would not want to ask God to take it away without giving that person a chance to respond to what God is trying to do in his life. When one realizes all that there is to be learned on the subject of healing, one can better understand why everyone who attends a *"faith healer's"* meeting is not healed or is not able to retain his healing.

If there were more teaching on the subject of healing in local churches, pastors probably would not see so many of their members going, even traveling long distances, hoping to find someone, somewhere, who could minister to their need. Jesus is probably the only one who ever did, or ever will have, a perfect healing ministry. Jesus had perfect faith in His Father's willingness to heal; He knew the condition of everyone's heart and life to which He ministered. He knew exactly what they needed to do to receive their healing and He was not afraid to tell them. He alone decided then, and decides now, what type of healing is best for each individual—instantaneous or gradual.

Chapter Seventeen

"Ultimate Healing"

O ccasionally, one hears Christians remark that someone for whose healing they had been praying for had received the "*ultimate*" healing. By that, they mean that the sick one did not receive their healing here on earth but died and went to heaven where there is, of course, no sickness. But is that really an answer that can be expected when one prays the prayer of faith mentioned in James 5:15? No. James says that the prayer of faith will save the sick and the Lord will *raise him up* (not kill him). Jesus said that those who believe in Him would lay hands on the sick and they would *recover (not die)*.

But, one might say, according to Hebrews 9:27, does there not come a time when everyone must die? Yes, except for those who are alive at the time of the rapture (II Thess 5:17). So one must compare scripture with scripture to gain a balanced understanding of God's truth. According to the many scriptures quoted elsewhere in this book, God has promised long and fruitful lives to those who live and walk in consistent obedience to Him. Therefore the truth to be arrived at here is that until one has lived out the *long days* that God has promised him, he can expect to be healed when he is sick.

How long might one expect to live if he follows God wholeheartedly? God has not chosen to tell most people (as He did Hezekiah in II Kings 20:6) the number of their days, but it seems resonable to assume that one who has lived most of his life in submission to God should expect, at the least, to live the calculated average life span according to the era and part of the world that he lives in.

Before the flood recorded in Genesis, men lived to be several hundred years old. After the flood, because of changes in the atmosphere caused by the flood and also changes in man's diet, the average life span shortened rapidly. By the time of David and Solomon, the average life span was 70 years (Ps. 90:10). Presently, the expected life span of those living in the United States is 68 years for men and 70 years for women. The very least one can expect, according to the scriptures, is to live to see his grandchildren (Ps. 128:6)

Regarding the idea that "ultimate" healing might be a possible answer to the prayer of faith, who would want to ask for healing if it meant that they *might* be healed as a result or they might die and go to heaven, especially if they had young children or were just beginning to discover God's plan for their lives?

The belief that God might heal in either one of the above ways destroys all hope, faith and expectancy that one will recover from their sickness. It cast doubt on God's promises and leaves one wavering between two possibilities (James 1:6-7). Even when one's days and purpose are fulfilled, one does not necessarily need to leave this world by means of a slow and agonizing illness. There is no scriptural basis for believing such a thing. There is no record of any of the Old or New Testament saints dying by a slow, agonizing disease. The Bible does say that the prophet Elisha died of a disease (II Kings 13:14). However, what disease he died of is not known. The Bible does not say if it was something that came upon his life suddenly and took his life quickly and mercifully or not. The Bible also says that by the mouth of two or three witness a matter shall be established (Matt. 18:16), so one cannot determine spiritual truth by one scripture, especially one that is vague and leaves one with more questions than it does answers.

It is hard to see how a slow agonizing death by a disease such as cancer, emphysema etc., with all the financial hardship and physical and emotional suffering such diseases cause to families can bring glory to God or testify to His goodness, faithfulness and power.

So how should one pray for those who are elderly and very ill? Should one pray for God to *"heal them or take them home"* as Christians sometimes do? Should one pray the *"heal them if it be Your will" prayer?*

Since one can't know the number of another person's days or even if their purpose on earth has been fulfilled, it is probably best to let God lead you in some situations. I always pray for healing unless God tells me otherwise. I do not try to decide the number of the sick persons days with my prayer. If one does not feel that he can pray the prayer of faith that James talks about because of the advanced age of the sick person, why not pray a petition prayer for healing. Who knows what God will do? James 4:2 says *"...you do not have because you do not ask."*

Many people, both young *and* old have been so ill, even in comas, that there has been no quality of life and no hope for recovery as far as the medical profession could see, yet God has raised them up in answer to believing prayer. No one is too old or too *"out of it"* for God to heal. My saintly aunt lived to be 108 years old. She did not die of sickness, she just went to sleep and never woke up again here on this earth.

177

I have a cousin whose elderly father became ill with cancer. He was a Christian and his family prayed that he might not die of cancer because most of the time that involves an extended time of suffering. God answered that prayer. His cancer went into remission, and he lived a normal life for quite awhile before dying quite suddenly and mercifully with what the doctors said was an aneurism. He was alive and well one moment and the next moment he was in heaven with God.

One minister said that she usually asks the sick person, "How would you like me to pray for you?" That is probably a good thing to do because the answer might help one to determine the state of mind of the sick person—for instance, whether he really wants to get well or is just giving up. If he is does not want to get well, he might benefit from some encouragement before prayer. Sometimes people of advanced age become weary of life's struggles and become homesick for heaven and their eternal rest. (Even doctors say that once people lose the will to live, it is difficult to bring them back to wholeness.)

One should never pray for God to take anyone "*home*" if it is not known whether or not the sick one is born again. Instead one should pray that if the person is not born again, God would give him the presence of mind and the opportunity to call upon God for salvation.

Many Christians are reluctant to pray for anyone's healing for fear that the sick one might not receive healing and then the pray-*er* will look foolish or powerless. Better for one to look that way than for someone to die because they had no one to intercede for them and encourage them to believe God for their healing.

The Christian's part in the healing of others is to pray and believe God with them for their healing. God's part is to do the healing. Probably not everyone one prays for will be healed (because of the hindrances that are written about in this book). However, if they *do* die of their sickness, at least the one praying and believing God for their healing and encouraging the sick one to do the same, will have the peace of knowing that it was not because *he* did not do all *he* could for that person.

Chapter Eighteen

God's Sovereignty

Some Christians erroneously attribute the sovereignty of God as one reason why God does not always heal, or desire to heal His children. To believe that God would withhold healing from one of His beloved, trusting children just to prove that He is boss, shows a lack of knowledge of God's word, His nature and His heart toward His children.

The fact that God is sovereign simply means that as Creator and sustainer of the universe and all that is within it, He is the Supreme Being of that universe. He has all power, is accountable to no one and can do what He pleases. *Yet Jesus makes it clear in His word that it is the Father's good pleasure to give His children the kingdom,* (Luke 12:32). *God, Himself also says that He will not withhold any good thing from those who walk uprightly* (Psalm 84:11).

Just as important as God's sovereignty (or maybe more) is His never changing, never failing word. Numbers

23:19 says,

> *"God is not a man that He should lie, nor a son of man that He should repent, has he said and will he not do it? Or has he spoken and will He not make it good?"*

In Isaiah 55:11 God says,

> *"So shall My word be that goes forth from my mouth; it shall not return unto Me void but it shall accomplish what I please and it shall prosper in the thing for which I sent it."*

I Kings 8:56 reads:

> *"...There has not failed one word of all His good promise..."*

II Cor. 1:20 reads:

> *"For all the promises of God are yes, and in Him, amen, to the glory of God through us."*

The Psalmist said, in Psalm 119:89:

"Forever, O Lord, Thy word is settled in heaven."

Matt. 24:35 reads:

"Heaven and earth shall pass away but My words will by no means pass away."

How can any of the things that God says about His word be trusted if one believes that it might be negated at any moment by a sovereign act of God? Where is the scriptural evidence for such a thing happening?

God has a very tender heart toward His children. Unlike some earthly fathers, God does not tease, taunt, frustrate or disappoint them. Psalm 103:13 says that the Lord pities those that fear Him and that His mercy toward them is from everlasting to everlasting.

He invites His children to come boldly before His throne to find mercy and grace to help in time of need (Hebrews 4:16) and in Luke 11:9-14, Jesus says *"...ask, and it will be given to you; seek, and you will find; knock, and it will be opened to you."* He also says that if His children ask Him for one thing,

He will not give them something else (verses 11-13).

To suggest that God, by a demonstration of His sovereignty, would fail to keep one of His promises to a child of God who has put all his hope and trust in Him and His word is to deny His word, His goodness, His faithfulness, His consistency, His integrity, and His commitment to His children.

Conclusion

Throughout this book, I have presented Biblical evidence that God wants us whole; body, soul and spirit and I have presented many reasons why some Christians fail to receive the healing they need or desire. I trust that those who falsely believe that God wills for some of us to be healed and for others to remain sick will prayerfully consider the scripture references given here.

A word of caution—we must be careful not to judge other Christians because we do not know for what reason or purpose sickness is present in anyone's life. (We are not called to judge our brother but to love him and pray for him and to encourage him. The only one we can rightly judge is ourselves and that we are called to do).

Our brother may have great faith and great obedience both, yet suffer an attack of illness. The more effective a person's ministry is, the harder Satan will work to destroy that person and his ministry.

The battle may be so fierce that reinforcements are needed, just as in a natural war. The Bible says, in Leviticus 26:8:

"Five of you shall chase a hundred, and a hundred of you shall put ten thousand to flight: your enemies shall fall by the sword before you."

I believe it is possible that many Christians have died before their time because they either did not know what the word of God teaches about healing or they did not receive the support and encouragement that they needed from their fellow Christians. This should not be.

Our sick brother or sister in Christ does not need someone telling him that he needs to accept his illness as his *"thorn-in-the-flesh"* and learn to bear it patiently. He needs someone to stand with him in prayer, believing God with him for his healing. God's word tells us to *"...pray for one another that [we] might be healed"* (James 5:16), not that we might accept our illness.

We Christians ought to so believe God's word and so desire to see His power and faithfulness manifested to the world that when one of our members is stricken with disease, we will stand together as a church family, praying, believing and claiming God's healing promises, perhaps even fasting as a body, until the sick one's healing comes.

Many Christians need to get a greater hold on the word of God. It is good to examine one's beliefs every so often and asks one's self these questions:

> "Do I believe what I do just because it is the traditional view of my denomination?" "Have I just heard people express certain opinions about spiritual things so often that I believe what they say without seeking confirmation from the word of God? ""Do I believe what I do because I am convinced that is what the word of God teaches?"

The Bible says in Romans 3:4, *"...let God be true, but every man a liar..."*

Every Christian has a responsibility to study the word of God for himself to see what God would say to him about his own situation, instead of relying on the opinions, views, interpretations, thoughts, experiences and even the research of others — *including those of this author.*

Christians also need to be careful not to let the things they *do not* know cause them to doubt the things they *do.*

187

This is a tactic of Satan to distract Christians from the *pure* truth of God's word. Satan and his messengers are responsible for seeing that certain scriptures are misread, misinterpreted, misapplied, ignored, or even forgotten. (Matt. 4:1-11 and Ps. 103:2).

Here is a good rule for interpreting scripture:

> When a abundance of scripture or scriptural passages seem to be in agreement concerning any one subject, yet there are one or two that seem to contradict the abundance, we need to re-examine our interpretation of the one or two. We do this by a more thorough study of the word of God on the subject at hand. When we do that, our study will usually result in an interpretation of the seemingly contradictory scriptures that is more in harmony with the rest of God's word.

God's word does not contradict itself but it does interpret itself.

If you need healing, you should study all that the Bible has to say about healing. When you are convinced that God wants you well, begin to claim His healing promises every day in prayer. As much as possible, avoid those who do not believe as you do about the biblical teaching on healing. (Eventually, their doubt can cause you to doubt, too). Also, as much as possible, find people that will agree to stand in prayer with you for your healing. Ask God to show you if you have any of the hindrances in your life that are mentioned in this book. Be willing to make any changes in your life (and attitudes) that the Lord may require of you. Be sure you are doing and being all that God has called you to do and be and that you are totally committed to him. Stay in an attitude of praise and thanksgiving and expectancy. Do not give up!! God honors consistency and perseverance. (James 5:16; Luke 18:1-8; Gal. 6:1-9).

"Let us hold fast the confession of our hope without wavering for He who promised is faithful."

Hebrew 10:2

Works Cited

Books

Bosworth, F. F. (1973). <u>christ the healer.</u> (8th ed.). (R. V. Bosworth, Ed.). Old Tappan, NJ: Fleming H. Revell Company. Cruden, A. (1930). <u>Cruden's complete concordance.</u> (A. D. Adams, C. H. Irwin, S. A. Waters, Ed.). Philadelphia, PA: The John C. Winston Company.

Harrison, E. F. (Ed.). (1971). <u>The Wycliffe bible commentary: new testament.</u> Chicago: Moody Press.

Buckingham, J. (1976). <u>Daughter of destiny Kathryn Kulhman...her story.</u> Plainfield, NJ: Logos International.

Lake, J. G. (1994). <u>John G Lake: his life, his sermons, his boldness of faith.</u> (W. Reidt, Ed.). Kenneth Copeland Publications: Fort Worth. Murray, A. (1982). <u>Divine healing.</u> New Kensington, PA: Whitaker House.

Osborn, Sr., T. L. (1959). <u>Healing the sick.</u> (20th Ed.). Tulsa, OK: T.L. Osborn Evangelistic Association. Simpson, A. B. (2007). <u>The gospel of healing.</u> Goodyear, AZ:

Diggory Press, Inc.

Strong, J. (1995, 1996). The new Strong's exhaustive concordance of the bible. Nashville: Thomas Nelson Publishers. Vine, W. E., Unger, M. F., White, Jr., W. (1984, 1996). Vine's complete expository dictionary. Nashville: Thomas Nelson, Inc. Yeomans, L. (2003). His healing power. Tulsa, OK: Harrison House.

Dictionaries

American heritage dictionary. (1994). (2nd Ed.). New York: Dell Publishing.

Flexner, S. B., Stein, J., Su, P.Y. (Ed.). (1980). The random house dictionary. New York: Random House.

Websites

Simpson, S. Biblical divine healing versus other types of healing. Retrieved April 15, 2009 from the World Wide Web: http://www.deceptioninthechurch/divine healing. html

Truth in History. Welsh revival of 1904-1905. Retrieved June 27, 2012 from the World Wide Web: http://www. truthinhistory.org/the-welsh-revival-of-1904-1905.html.

.

Appendix

RECOMMENDED READING

<u>Christ the Healer</u>

F.F. Bosworth

Fleming H. Revell Co.

<u>Divine Healing</u>

Andrew Murray

Whitaker House

<u>The Gospel of Healing</u>

A.B. Simpson

Diggory Press, Inc.

<u>Let Go and Let God</u>

Albert E. Cliffe

Prentiss Hall Inc.

God Can Heal You Now

Emily Gardner Neal

Prentiss Hall Inc.

Healing the Sick

T.L. Osborn

T.L. Osborn Evangelistic Association

John G. Lake

His Life, His Sermons, His Boldness of Faith

W. Reidt

Kenneth Copeland Publications

The Nearly Perfect Crime

Francis MacNutt

Chosen Books

A division of Baker Publishing Group

His Healing Power

Dr. Lillian Yeomans

Harrison House

CPSIA information can be obtained at www.ICGtesting.com
Printed in the USA
LVOW040943260912

300373LV00001B/3/P